the CITY gardener
Urban Oasis

the CITY gardener Urban Oasis

Matt James

For everyone who
had a hand in this

First published in 2004 by Collins
an imprint of HarperCollins*Publishers*
77–85 Fulham Palace Road,
London W6 8JB

The Collins website is:
www.**collins**.co.uk

See page 224 for full picture credits

Matt James photographs: Nikki English

Editor: Helen Ridge
Designer: Alison Fenton

For HarperCollins
Senior Managing Editor: Angela Newton
Editor: Alastair Laing
Editorial Assistant: Lisa John
Design Manager: Luke Griffin
Production Controller: Chris Gurney

A CIP catalogue record for this book
is available from the British Library

ISBN 0007176287

Colour reproduction by Colourscan
Printed and bound in Great Britain by
The Bath Press

CONTENTS

INTRODUCTION

I wasn't born a gardener; no one is. I thought gardening was a sport for 'older people' in tweed jackets and kneeling pads. Then the bug bit, followed by college, nursery and landscape work, university, teaching and now a TV series! Something I never would've imagined.

Gardening is big business today, and a rapidly changing industry with a whole set of myths growing up around it. Some say it's too prescribed, and that a simple back-to-nature pastime has become 'sexed-up'. Sexy – yes, I'll agree with that! – gardening is one of the most basic activities there is, and we definitely seem genetically programmed to want to do it!

There's nothing I like more than propagating my favourite tree, or packing a container with fat lily bulbs as I look forward to the scent and splendour to come. I love looking at plants; I'm curious about how they tick. I love planting them, watching them grow and flower.

I love playing with designs, too. There are so many possibilities to turn a city backyard into a tiny paradise that I sometimes want to do all of them at once. Thank goodness for clients who have their own ideas, so that I'm forced to rein in my excitement. Working to a brief means I don't go gaga over having too much to choose from!

And yet… I have the tiniest space imaginable for my garden. I live in London with a garden 'up there' on a balcony. I get my digging fix at college or my Mum's, but I don't feel downhearted. I've learned that you can garden anywhere; even a window box can be your own little acre. And we all know the saying, 'nice things come in small packages'!

In this book, I've tried to do two things: to lead you further down the garden path (!) and throw in some interesting and helpful facts to make that journey easier.

The first book, *The City Gardener*, was written to hopefully inspire you, to get you off your sofa and believe in yourself: you, too, could have a garden as good as any you might see on TV. And you'd be creating it all by yourself. This volume moves on… gently, I hope, because having tweaked your interest I don't want to burden you with tales of how hard it is to make a garden – because it simply isn't!

It's said the devil is in the detail… but we're gonna make a friend of him! I begin at the beginning: how to see your space, and what you might do with it. There's information on gardening styles in the second chapter; this helps you to further define what you like. Hard landscaping isn't everyone's cup of tea – no wonder so many books skirt around it! I've tried to show you the value of a good set of garden bones: building a patio or putting down a deck yourself can be really satisfying and a source of pride. Paths are often neglected, too – seen purely as a means of getting from A to B – when they are really a valuable part of the design itself.

Some of the plants I love, many of which I used in the *The City Gardener* programme, you'll find in the fourth chapter. This monster chapter is the fulcrum of the book. Plants are the exciting and surprising part of any garden. Dip in and use this chapter to map out combinations that work well together. There's also some handy info on actually buying your plants – how do you know if you've been sold a dud or not?

People are always puzzled when it comes to 'what goes with what' in their planting schemes. So, in the fifth chapter, I've included the key things that I think about – and some useful combos that work. And there's help with how you actually plant your choice specimens. Browse through the plant lists in the final chapter. There are some unusual categories here, and you're bound to find many different plants for your garden – sun or shade. They'll help to make planning your garden a lot easier and, dare I say it, fun!

Yes. Fun. I wouldn't want to do anything in my spare time that bored me. Would you? What else helps get you fit, gets you out in the sun, gives you something lovely to look at that changes with the seasons, provides food (!) and gives you that all-important space outside to chill out in the summer evening sun?

So, get creative in this busy world. And enjoy your gardening!

ARM YOURSELF!

Most of us are impulse buyers when it comes to gardening. We go to the garden centre or nursery, see a pot of lilies in bloom or a rose whose scent we like, take it home, and find ourselves faced with the dilemma of just where in the garden to plant it.

There's nothing wrong with that; we all learn by our own mistakes and successes, but the downside is that pretty soon we find ourselves with a collection of plants that don't fit in the garden. I'm sure you've been there! The *Buddleia* has become a monster, the *Rhododendron* always looks sick (pity we didn't realise it needs an acid soil to thrive in), the *Forsythia* now blocks all the light from the kitchen window, and we wish we'd planted evergreens on the boundary instead of deciduous trees because in winter our neighbours have a bird's-eye view into the kitchen. Worse still, having had the enjoyment of buying the plant, we just don't get round to planting it because we haven't got a plan, and rearranging the garden for our latest purchase is just too much hassle. I've seen a lot of plants, which have never been planted out, still standing in their pots, sulking in a corner, pot-bound, neglected and dying, because the garden simply isn't ready for new acquisitions. This is where a little planning comes in handy.

MAKING PLANS

Planning doesn't have to be daunting, with fancy drawings and measurements in scale to the last millimetre. It can be very simple, **just a sketch and some lists.** It'll focus you on what you actually want and need from your outer space, and eliminate follies like the helicopter pad! Once you have a rough plan, you can then buy plants with confidence, knowing that they'll fit into the garden. The important thing here is to actually make a plan.

PLANNING WILL HELP YOU FOCUS ON YOUR WANTS AND NEEDS

NICE 'N' EASY DOES IT

I encourage you to take it slowly. I know we've all seen TV makeovers where spaces are instantly transformed, and the presenters work to a frantic deadline, but we don't have to work up such a sweat! These programmes show just what can be done with the shabbiest plot, and aim to inspire us by uncovering the whole process from terrible beginnings to blooming paradise. For real-life gardeners, though, the process should be gentler, mirroring the natural transformative processes at work in nature. It's so much easier on us to do it this way, too.

Doing the garden doesn't have to cost thousands, really. And even if you do have a modest budget, it doesn't all have to be spent in one go. Taking on the work yourself and taking your time makes the whole process totally satisfying, and allows you to do it according to your wallet and your energy. The key is to **prioritise the tasks**.

Keep reminding yourself that your garden is much more than a 'quick fix' and, to be honest, you'll never actually finish it. Like your personal taste, gardens evolve, and not always into something of great beauty and personal triumph. Sometimes they become a source of frustration. But when that happens don't despair – that's gardening. Getting a plan together, however, should make the design process as painless as possible, and smooth out those times when frustration would otherwise set in.

QUESTION TIME

So begin slowly. Cast an eye over the space you want to transform. **Take your time**, sit, look around you, walk the space, view the garden from different perspectives. What can you see from the window? Where do you naturally gravitate to in summer to make the most of the late-afternoon sun? And if it's too hot, where do you seek shade? Go to the end of the garden and stand on the boundary, looking back at the house. How might you knit the character of the house into the garden? Are there any features you'd rather not see? Which place gives you the most privacy from neighbours, or prevents you from being overlooked?

Look at any **existing trees and shrubs**, and consider keeping and incorporating them into your design. What would the space feel like if those plants weren't there? Curb the urge to immediately dig everything up and start with a bare garden; you may well regret such enthusiasm later!

FUNCTIONAL NECESSITIES

It's so easy to fantasise about having a beautiful space, but the boring bits need to figure somewhere in the equation, too. We live practical lives in small spaces, and need to consider the functions the garden has to fulfil. Everyone has a rubbish bin, and you'll want to hide it, but you'll also want to be able to get at it easily, as well as have easy access to the street for collection. Sometimes we need to provide space for the car, or an area where the children can play safely. And what about the washing line or the rotary dryer? Functional necessities should be considered before we start to dream about plants and alfresco dining!

Make a rough sketch, and factor in these considerations. Remember to take account of the obvious, such as the fact that a retractable washing line looks better than a whirligig, but don't forget that you still need space around the line for the washing to dry. The last thing you want is the drying area to be so small that your silk shirts get snagged on the roses, or to see your choice lilies decapitated when a towel catches a gust of wind.

PRIORITY CHECK

List and prioritise all the items and functions that you consider essential, such as:

- car port
- bike store
- toddlers' play area
- washing line/rotary dryer
- rubbish bins/wheelie bins
- garden compost bins/kitchen waste bins
- recycling boxes
- access to drains and services (manhole covers)
- screening for an oil tank
- pet hutches

Sharon & Gordon's garden, Glasgow

DESIRABLE FEATURES

Once the unavoidable necessities have been dealt with, move on to the more aesthetic features. Get the family together and draw up a list of their 'wants' for the garden. Ultimately the wants and desires of everybody may not be satisfied – some may not be feasible or indeed affordable – but at least everyone has their say. The great thing about a family free-for-all is that it'll whet everyone's appetite. With luck they'll want to muck in and lend a hand, easing the pressure on you and making the whole process more enjoyable. Remember that some things may be able to perform a dual role, for example a place for sunbathing might double up as a play area for the kids.

WISH LIST

The features that you'd like your garden to have may include some of the following:

- lawned area for sunbathing
- covered area for chilling out
- sand-pit with cover
- paddling pool
- pond, water feature, fountain
- area for a swing
- built-in barbecue
- hot tub/Jacuzzi
- patio
- dining area with table and chairs
- permanent seating areas
- garden benches
- shed/greenhouse
- children's play house/tree house
- sun house/gazebo

Tanith & Kay's garden, Bristol

LIFESTYLE

How you lead your life is going to have a big impact on any garden design, and there are a number of 'do you' questions that will help you with the planning process.

DO YOU...

- use the garden in winter or only in summer?
- make use of the garden during the day, or at evenings and weekends only?
- enjoy alfresco dining? Only at weekends, or also in the evenings?
- have any children? Are they toddlers wanting sand-pits or boys playing with footballs? Toddlers and open ponds can be a dangerous combination.
- want to encourage wildlife into the garden?
- have a small home office or work from home?
- dry washing outside?
- like plants? Are you a plant-aholic?
- hate mowing the lawn? (in which case, don't factor in a lawn)
- want a totally secluded space for sunbathing *au naturel*?
- have a hot tub or outdoor Jacuzzi?
- want an outdoor swimming pool? Exercise area?
- want something in flower 24/7/365?
- positively enjoy gardening?
- want to grow vegetables or fruit?
- have a dog or other pets that will use the garden?
- want a garden just to look out on? (you'll want a picture window)
- spend a lot of time away from home? (you'll need a self-watering system for pots)
- want an outside space for DIY, fixing bikes, motorbikes, etc?
- or any of your family/friends have a disability?
- hate garden maintenance? (you're looking for a garden that looks after itself)
- want secluded areas to hide away in and chill out?

LOCALITY

Your garden isn't an island. It's affected by its surroundings and this will influence both how you use it and what you can grow. In a seaside garden, for example, plants need to be able to resist salt-laden wind, which will burn the leaves of more delicate plants. The city has a different set of problems: air pollution from traffic, smells, noise, rubbish and grime, not to mention the need for increased security. Think about these factors and the likely impact they will have on what you want to do in the garden. Work out how, through some clever design and thoughtful planting, you can minimise some of the negative aspects of urban living. For example, running water or a tall stand of *Miscanthus sacchariflorus* rustling in the wind can help to **mask the sounds of a busy road**. If you're worried about intruders, why not plant a tall spiky hedge of holly or hawthorn? It'll look a lot better than rows of razor wire and be just as effective.

VIEWS

A view is simply what you can see from your property. It may include your garden but it's bound to include someone else's! Think outside the box of your own space. If your neighbour has beautiful trees in his backyard, visually 'borrow' them to add to your own picture – you'll see them every time you look at your own garden, so you'll be enjoying a bonus for nothing. In many cases, borrowing scenery will actually make a small space feel much larger. In particular, the view from frequently used rooms like the kitchen and living room will be important. If you look out onto a church, for instance, don't block the view with ill-placed planting. Instead, why not frame it with structural clipped box (*Buxus sempervirens*) or mirror its tall spire with conical-shaped trees? Keep the desirables and make focal points of them. However, you may need to disguise an ugly shed or divert attention away from an electricity substation by **careful screening** and the use of studied perspectives.

THE HARD BITS

Repair the fences that are your responsibility before you start to implement your design. If your neighbour's boundary fences are in poor repair, try to negotiate for them to do the work. Otherwise, create a new boundary fence just inside the decrepit one – but on your land.

If walls or paving are on their last legs, see if they can be repaired without costing a fortune. But use common sense; a crumbling wall can easily be an eyesore, whereas a folly 'ruin' can be immensely charming. Dilapidated hard landscaping will detract from even the most beautiful garden;

it'll make you notice what's wrong, and distract from what's right. Sometimes an old structure has to be demolished because it would cost too much to repair or replace. But old materials can add considerable charm to a garden, so if you can't leave them in place, at least try to recycle them.

Simply identifying and then ignoring a potential problem can easily cause heartache in the long term, especially when a bunch of workmen with their size 9s trample over your prized herbaceous border! So take remedial action before getting stuck into major replanting.

Bhavana & Nigel's garden, Leicester

EXISTING PLANTS

Consider moving large specimen plants if they are in the wrong place, but try not to ditch them completely. Mature plants are invaluable and they take years to grow to that size. Look at them as an asset; they'll give a sense of permanence and maturity to a new design. Those shrubs on the boundary may serve a **useful purpose** (it could be that they're screening an eyesore), and might need only a little pruning, not complete removal. It's relatively easy to remove a shrub or tree, but impossible to replace it with something of equal stature that fulfils the original function. That's particularly the case with trees – you won't know what you're missing with a tree until it's no longer there! Do avoid those cowboys who call themselves 'tree-care specialists'. Anyone can look macho with a chainsaw, but only a trained arboriculturalist knows how trees grow, and how to thin and prune them properly.

Just moved? If you can, wait a whole year to see what will emerge during that time. There may be some very pleasant surprises. When you inherit a mature garden, do try to **resist the urge** to make changes straight away. While the garden you have inherited might appear lifeless during the winter months, come summer it is just as likely to be full of riotous colour. A few strategically placed evergreens could be all that's needed. If you must move mature plants, do it between autumn and early spring, and try to move as much soil with the roots as possible. This way you can trick the plant into feeling it hasn't been moved, and it'll re-establish better. With existing perennials, it's possible to lift, divide and move them out of harm's way. Watch out for bulbs, too. Lift and store them in a dry place, then replant them into your final design.

WHAT ABOUT THE WEEDS?

Some weeds are almost virtuous and garden-worthy. Most, alas, are not. Ground elder and bindweed are the gardener's hell. I don't like using chemicals, but in these cases a translocated weedkiller like 'Round Up' might be necessary – it'll kill the roots and all. An environmentally friendly way to deal with weeds is to hire a flame gun and sweep over the area, but perennial weeds will still reappear and therefore need to be sprayed or dug out by hand (don't compost these – bin them). Sorry, that's a thankless task, but nothing that can't be helped along by a few beers and a few friends. Annual weeds can be pulled up without bother or simply dug in; just try to prevent them seeding themselves. And don't forget: make friends with your hoe!

You can avoid the chore of weeding established flower beds by regularly mulching around your plants with cocoa shell, compost, bark or gravel. It's best to **weed little and often**, and try to regard it as a meditation rather than a grim back-breaking task.

THE BROWN STUFF

There are many types of soil, from heavy clay, through silt, to sand. Clay soil feels sticky in your hand and forms a ball. Sandy soil feels gritty and will have a 'rasping' sound. If, when you rub your soil between thumb and forefinger, it 'squeaks' a bit and feels soapy, then it has a high proportion of silt. Peaty soils are practically black, as they're almost entirely made up of decomposed organic matter; they soak up water like a sponge.

WHAT TYPE OF SOIL?

As well as the soil's physical characteristics, try to find out the basic chemical nature of your soil, or its pH – this is another factor influencing the range of plants you can grow successfully. Visual observation is the easiest way; look at the plants your neighbours are growing. *Rhododendron*, *Camellia* and heathers all signify an acid soil, whereas *Clematis* and *Buddleia* thrive on alkaline soils. If you have a chalky soil, it's unquestionably going to be alkaline. The most accurate way of measuring the pH is to get a **pH soil-testing kit** from your local garden centre and follow the instructions. Just make sure the soil sample you take is typical of your whole garden. Don't grab a handful from where you've recently had a bonfire, spilt fertiliser or mixed cement – it'll throw the reading way out. It's a good idea to take pH readings from several different locations around your garden as they can vary dramatically over a relatively small area.

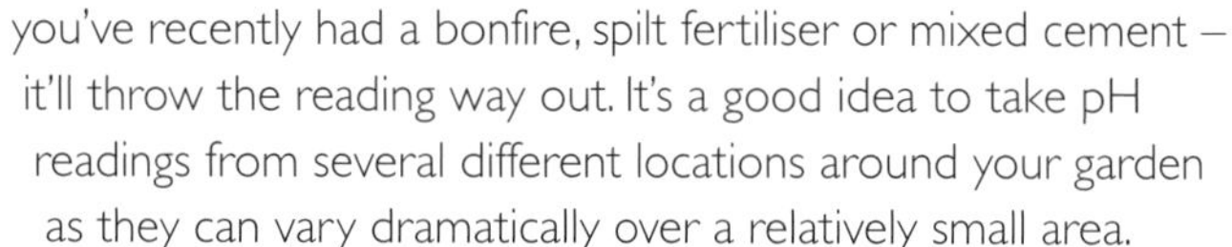

Once you know the pH of your soil, don't fight it, but select plants that will do well without much tinkering – trying to alter your soil's pH (for example, by adding buckets of pine needles to an alkaline soil in the hope that you can grow *Rhododendron*) is a waste of time and money. The choice of plants that like acid or alkaline soils is huge, so you'll never feel deprived. If you must grow acid-lovers on an alkaline soil, simply grow them in pots or raised beds filled with ericaceous (lime-free) compost.

Signs of a poor soil include water sitting on the surface, stunted plants or the feeling that you're hacking through concrete when you stick your spade in. It's a good idea to dig exploratory holes in several places around your plot just to find the areas of both good and lousy soil. Not many of us want to remove the soil we've got (it's a job and a half, believe me!), so look upon your soil as a matrix to which you can make many improvements. The perfect soil is that elusive thing most gardeners spend years striving for. But don't despair; plants are plucky and will do well in less than ideal conditions.

TOPSOIL & SUBSOIL

If you're undertaking major earthworks, keep the topsoil and subsoil separate – this is most important. The topsoil (if you have it) is usually darker in colour, more friable and about 15cm (6in) deep. Below that will be a lighter-coloured, more compacted layer, which is the subsoil. Topsoil is where plants get the food and water they need, and is a hive of bacterial activity, which helps plants to grow. Its darker colour is due to the humus content. Think of subsoil as the supporting foundations of a house – essential, but not the part you can live in. Subsoil has few nutrients. If you are digging out an area, save the topsoil. Set it to one side while you excavate the subsoil. In newly built houses, the gardens often have little or no topsoil at all, just builder's rubble covered with subsoil; in this case you'll need to buy in lorry-loads of topsoil. Or, if you're a lazy gardener like me, you can always grow your plants in containers.

WHAT IS GOOD SOIL?

Good soil has quite a few distinctive qualities. It's dark in colour (from copious additions of organic matter), **light and pleasant to dig**, and moist without being waterlogged. It drains easily, has a good population of earthworms, does not bake like concrete in summer, and does not form a hard crust, which makes water penetration difficult.

Add nutrients and humus to the topsoil, where all the activity takes place. The best way is to add masses of bulky well-rotted animal manure, spent hops or garden compost. Fork this in to the top 15cm (6in). Add a sprinkle of seaweed meal, and watch everything grow.

It is a myth that the yearly digging of your soil will improve it. Vegetable gardeners tend to turn over their plots each year, saying that pests are exposed to the birds and that the soil is loosened up. Yet there are also no-dig gardeners who simply add layers of **organic matter** to the surface of the soil, maybe just forking it into the top 8cm (3in), and they do nothing more than remove the odd perennial weed. If you think about it, this is the way nature does things... by dropping leaves that decompose naturally and refertilise the soil. It's up to you which system you prefer, but I suspect you'll have to do some digging to begin with. In an established bed, there's no need to dig (if you do, you'll damage roots or spear those bulbs you planted last year); just mulch with organic matter and the worms will pull it in, doing your digging for you.

ACCESS

A city gardener with ambitious plans for his/her garden, but with no rear access, is asking for a headache. Your best friend here is a tape measure. Don't take the risk of ordering bulky items without measuring doorways or passageways first, as *everything* may need to be taken through the house and out through the back door. Conveyors can be used to speed things up, and you'll need a sturdy ramp if you have steps up to the front door (and the same at the back door, too). It's a good idea to remove all fixtures and fittings that might get in the way if you're using a wheelbarrow to ferry stuff through the house; and check that the wheelbarrow *itself* will go through. If you've bought mature trees, consider how you're going to get them into the garden. Will they bend successfully around tight, awkward corners?

Think about **access for lorries** delivering soil and building materials, especially if you need to organise parking for them on the street. If you want to get a hot-tub into your garden, you may need to hire a crane to swing it over the roof.

To make life easier for yourself, pop along to your local hire shop, tell them what your problem is, and ask them to come up with a solution.

TOPOGRAPHY

Having things level can be vital. We only have to climb the Tower of Pisa to see what a relatively small lean can do to our senses: we might be going up the stairs one step at a time but some of the time we are walking on the level, which is enough to throw our sense of balance completely askew. When it comes to laying a patio, you want it to be fairly level: a 3m (10ft) patio with a 3cm (1in) slope away from the house is perfect, but an inch out on a raised pond with a formal edging looks awful as the water will drain away over one edge.

Topography – the lie of the land, to you and me – is the key to getting things level in the garden. So before that grand design gets you running off to hire a bulldozer or concrete mixer, it's a good idea to come to grips with the changes of levels in the area you intend to modify. Unlike a map-maker's job of surveying the Lakeland fells and the like, this is relatively easy to do. A few pegs, some string, a builder's level, some lengths of straight timber, and there is little you can't survey in your own backyard. And this is where you start to get a real feel for what you are planning: unless you are particularly skilled in scale drawings, you won't appreciate the size and scope of your vision until it's measured out on the ground with string, spray paint or chalk, and with heights marked out by lengths of bamboo or cheap roofing battens.

Before planning ponds, patios, walls, fences, pergolas, etc., you need to check the orientation of any slopes in the garden. If a slope is south-facing, this will provide the perfect home for tender sun-lovers (a bit like the south-facing slopes in wine-growing regions, cosseting those precious vineyards). If you build a wall with an east–west orientation, though, there'll be a cold shady area on the north-facing side, as well as a hot sunny area on the south-facing side of the wall.

When building a wall, or making a high raised bed, it's useful to consider the height of the sun relative to the season: a low wall might cast practically no shade in summer, but come winter its shade might cover most of the garden. And check out the **prospective views** from what you are about to build: the orientation of any planned structure needs to take into account what that structure is going to look out onto. Rather than having a south-facing sun trap looking straight into your neighbours' garden, you might decide on a chic west-facing dining area looking out over your pond instead.

CLIMATE

Apart from the generalised regional climate we live in, every garden has numerous localised climates that affect what we can grow; these are all directly linked to the garden's aspect and the orientation of the boundaries (the direction they face). Other factors that help create these different microclimates include the topography, such as a warm south-facing slope, the prevailing wind direction and force, such as an exposed dry easterly aspect, and the temperature, such as an area backed by a sun-baked south-facing wall or hidden behind a cold north-facing wall. Small microclimates also occur under overhanging trees (dry shade), up against a house wall (very dry) or next to ponds and streams (damp shade to damp sunny). Generally speaking, if you are near the coast, you will have a warmer microclimate with fewer extremes, as the sea loses and gains heat much more slowly than the land.

Apart from creating small specialised **microclimates** to suit certain plants, perhaps by tempering the wind with trellis, hedges, etc., it usually pays to work with what you already have. Fighting nature, even localised nature, often works out costly and extremely difficult.

ASPECT

The orientation of your garden dictates what plants will thrive there, simply because the direction a garden faces affects how much light it'll receive. A scorching-hot south-facing slope won't suit plants that like moist dappled shade. But it will make a good area for sunbathing or planting spectacular sun-lovers like *Canna* lilies, *Agapanthus* or even your own little vineyard.

The aspect of your garden is **easy to suss** a cheap compass will tell you where south is and, in fact, so will your watch – the sun is directly due south at one o'clock BST (British Summer Time). Once you know where south is, you'll be able to work out the orientation of your boundaries accordingly. But knowing the garden's aspect isn't everything. The seasons will also affect how much sunlight any particular garden receives. In midsummer, even a north-facing plot might receive some direct sunlight, early and late in the day.

Sit outside and see how much sun your garden gets at different times of the day. How much shade does your own house cast on the garden during the summer months as well as in winter? Where is the sunniest spot for summer lounging? Where are the shady corners for cool retreats when the midsummer sun gets just too much?

FACING NORTH

A northerly aspect is the most inhospitable for plants (and for us humans, come to think of it). It's characterised by almost perpetual shade, cool in summer, cold or **very cold in winter**, but it has a good steady light unless heavily shaded (which is why artists' studios generally face north). Soil beneath a north-facing wall tends to be dry and cold. You'll need to protect plants from winter winds. While it sounds like doom and gloom, it's not. Many plants like ferns, *Hosta*, bluebells (*Hyacinthoides non-scripta*), foxgloves (*Digitalis*), Christmas box (*Sarcococca*) and *Skimmia* positively loathe sunny spots and are therefore perfect for north-facing walls and fences.

FACING SOUTH

South-facing gardens generally have warm winters and very hot summers. Initially this sounds great, but plants can quickly suffer from **sun-scorch and drought**, so go for real hot-sun-lovers or incorporate loads of humus-rich material into the soil to retain moisture.

PLANTS FOR NORTHERLY ASPECTS

Aconitum•*Camellia*•*Cotoneaster*•*Cyclamen*•ferns•*Garrya elliptica*•*Hydrangea petiolaris* (climbing hydrangea)•*Jasminum nudiflorum* (winter jasmine)•*Lonicera* x *tellmanniana* (honeysuckle)•*Mahonia*•*Parthenocissus*•*Prunus cerasus* 'Morello' (morello cherry) •*Pyracantha*•*Ribes* (flowering currants, gooseberries)

Dicksonia antartica (tree fern)

Passiflora caerulea (passionflower)

FACING EAST

East-facing gardens are generally cool, can be bitter in winter, and warm and dry in summer. Plants, especially evergreens, in east-facing spots generally suffer from wind- and frost-damage, particularly in early spring. Plants that suit this aspect are the same as those for north-facing gardens, but you'll need to shade both magnolias and camellias from early morning sun in winter (their flowers can be harmed during frosty weather). Protect plants, too, from **desiccating winter winds**.

FACING WEST

West-facing gardens are similar to those that face south, but without the extremes – some gardeners even say 'west is best'. Apart from those that demand shade, **most plants will thrive**, especially more tender ones like *Actinidia*, *Akebia*, *Azara*, *Dahlia*, *Eremurus*, *Euphorbia*, *Lilium*, *Magnolia*, *Nicotiana*, *Salvia*, *Viola* and, of course, roses.

PLANTS FOR SOUTHERLY ASPECTS

Abutilon • *Agapanthus* • *Amaryllis belladonna* • *Callistemon* • *Campsis* • *Ceanothus* • *Cestrum* • *Chimonanthus* • *Cistus* • *Clematis* • *Cytisus battandieri* • *Hebe* • *Hoheria* • *Jasminum* (jasmine) • *Leptospermum* • *Narcissus* • *Nerine* • *Passiflora* (passionflower) • *Wisteria* • most fruit trees (apples, apricots, sweet cherries, figs, peaches, pears, plums, etc.)

SERVICES

Running under the ground are a host of hidden cables and pipes. These can contain anything from *EastEnders* (your cable TV hook-up) to the most important ingredient for the next cuppa (water from the mains pipe), not to mention gas or electricity. So, before wielding your spade or revving up that newly hired mini-JCB, it makes sense to find out where these services run.

The most obvious indicators to underground services are signs and inspection covers. Simply lift the manhole covers and note the direction in which the pipework runs. Subsidence, or strips of different-coloured concrete in a driveway, are also **useful pointers**. If you're new to the property, contact your local council or surveyor; they'll be able to offer help with detailed maps and plans.

If you draw a blank, hire a 'cable avoidance tool' (CAT for short) for piece of mind. It's a complete hand-held sonar system that you sweep over the ground and it 'beeps' back at you if there's a cable or pipe underneath. Then just mark your findings on the ground using spray paint or horticultural sand, so you can take extra care when digging.

Try to note the position of the following: manholes, drains, ventilation bricks, septic tank covers, underground telephone, water, power and TV cables, overhead telephone and power cables. Finding them the hard way, when laying a new path or planting a mature tree, can be costly and time-consuming, not to mention embarrassing!

WATER SUPPLY

With the changes to our weather brought on by global warming, it would probably be a good idea to install an outside tap to ease the burden of watering. This is quite easy to do; most DIY outfits sell simple kits containing all you need (apart from the hole in the wall). And if you are planning to do a bit of hard landscaping, installing a tap earlier rather than later makes a lot of sense: you will have water available for all that concrete mixing.

Once you have easy access to water, you might want to incorporate a **simple irrigation system**. Laying lengths of soaker hose (perforated hose that seeps water) throughout the drier beds in the garden means the plants will have easy access to all the water they need. Into the bargain, you will use a lot less water than if you sprinkle it on the surface of the soil – there, most of it will evaporate, whereas a soaker hose will deliver the water direct to the plant roots. What's more, all of this takes place out of sight, covered by soil or mulch. You could also hook an irrigation system up to a timer, to give you complete piece of mind, especially if you're away from home a lot.

Other automatic irrigation systems are also available, especially the types you often see in nurseries where small-bore tubing is run above ground and delivers the right amount of water to each plant via controllable taps. Such a system is particularly suited to the container-intensive garden, where much of the mechanics of the irrigation system can be concealed behind the planters.

LEGISLATION & PROTECTED ZONES

Check before removing any tree that it isn't subject to a Tree Preservation Order; phone your local council to check. And if your neighbour has a particularly noteworthy tree that benefits the neighbourhood, why not approach your council to allocate it TPO status? This way you can help preserve the identity of an area, something that takes time to develop and yet can so easily be ruined in half an hour by someone thoughtlessly removing a beautiful focal point.

If you live in an Area of Outstanding Natural Beauty (AONB), there might be local by-laws restricting what you can or can't do to your garden and garden 'furniture'. In some localities, trees with bright yellowish-green foliage like *Robinia pseudoacacia* 'Frisia' are outlawed, or building a pergola in the front garden might not be allowed. The same is true of Sites of Special Scientific Interest (SSSI) and Sites of Special Archaeological Significance (SSAS).

If you live in a conservation area, or your home is a listed building, or even if any of the features in your garden are listed, then you need to take the advice of your local council as to what you can and can't do. In conservation areas particularly, it is not a matter of whether your house and grounds have much in the way of outstanding period features, but the fact that it is part and parcel of a larger scheme, and altering one part of the scheme alters the whole. But as long as your approach to the garden is sympathetic to the area, your local council should have no objection to your plans.

Note the word 'sympathetic'. This is a key word when planning any alteration to your garden and house. Ideally, you want the two to enhance each other, and improve the area you live in. Planning in sympathy with your environment often gives the most successful approach to garden design.

As a rule of thumb, contact your council if you're considering building any large structures, as you may need planning permission; you'll also need permission for a roof terrace if this is not already designated for use. And don't forget to take your neighbours' views into consideration: let's face it, siting your garage so that it blocks your neighbour's view of the park/sea/lake/hillside won't do much in the neighbour-relations department!

PUTTING IT DOWN ON PAPER

This checklist, which you can enlarge on a photocopier, will help you look at your space in an organised way. It will help tie down what you and your family actually want and need from your garden and, coupled with a site plan, will help you define any design ideas. Tick your answers in the circles.

WHO USES THE GARDEN? (include pets)

name ______________________ age ______

name ______________________ age ______

name ______________________ age ______

name ______________________ age ______

WHICH DIRECTION DOES THE GARDEN FACE?

____

WHEN IS THE GARDEN MAINLY USED?

spring ○ summer ○ autumn ○ winter ○ all year ○

DESIRED CHARACTER/FEEL/MOOD OF GARDEN

formal ○ informal ○ grand ○ intimate ○ modern ○ traditional ○ cottage ○ other ○

____

PLANTING EMPHASIS

foliage/stem effect ○ flowers ○ fruit ○ vegetables ○ general year-round interest ○ seasonal interest: spring ○ summer ○ autumn ○ winter ○

FAVOURITE PLANTS TO BE INCLUDED

____

____

____

____

____

WHAT FEATURES DO YOU WANT/NEED?

lighting ○ irrigation ○ garden bench ○ picnic table and chairs (how many?) ○ umbrella ○ pond ○ fountain ○ ornaments ○ car parking ○ lawn ○ communal seating area ○ private/secluded seating area ○ sun terrace/patio ○ hot tub/Jacuzzi ○ children's play area ○ Wendy/tree house ○ sand pit ○ vegetable garden ○ herb garden ○ fruit garden ○ greenhouse ○ BBQ area ○ rubbish bin ○ storage ○ recycling boxes ○ washing line/ rotary dryer ○ tool/storage shed ○ compost heap/bin ○ other ○

____

____

____

____

ANY EXISTING PROBLEMS (visual and functional)

____

____

____

____

ELEMENTS/FEATURES TO BE RETAINED

____

____

____

____

ELEMENTS/FEATURES TO BE IMPROVED

___

ELEMENTS/FEATURES THAT DEFINITELY MUST GO

___

DESIRED LEVEL OF MAINTENANCE
daily ○ weekends ○ absolute minimum ○ other ○

___

PREFERRED LANDSCAPING MATERIALS
brick ○ gravel ○ cobbles ○ natural stone ○
concrete ○ setts ○ steel ○ iron ○ timber ○
decking ○ comments ___

EASE OF ACCESS TO GARDEN
(for lorry, van, skip, trees, etc.)

___

HOUSE
style and age ___
condition ___
façade materials ___
location of doors and windows ___

EXTERIOR FEATURES
any soil erosion? ___
heights of walls/fences ___
height of steps ___

EXISTING PLANTS (location and condition)

___

LEGISLATION & PROTECTED ZONES
(contact local council if any of the following apply)
Tree Preservation Order (TPO) ○ Area of Outstanding Natural Beauty (AONB) ○ Site of Special Scientific Interest (SSSI) ○ Site of Special Archaeological Significance (SSAS) ○ Listed building ○

WHAT WORK CAN I DO MYSELF?

___

WHAT WORK NEEDS A CONTRACTOR?

___

BUDGET ___
comments ___

TIMESCALE ___

NOTES ___

Newcastle

It's not a garden.
It's a parking space!

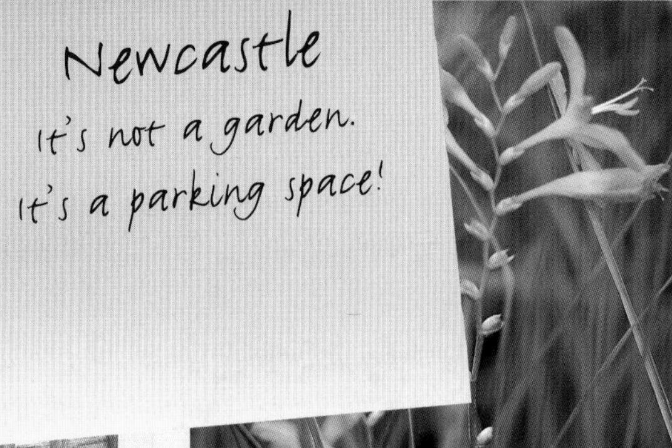

You don't need to be an electrician to install these lights. Any idiot can do it!

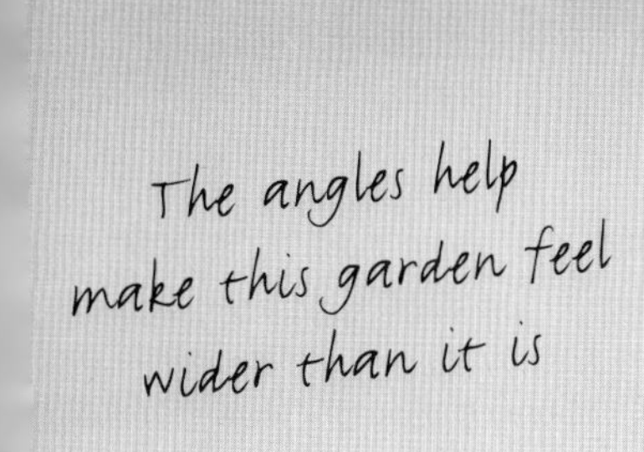

The angles help make this garden feel wider than it is

NEWCASTLE

Ian, a bachelor solicitor, made a plea for an ultra easy-to-care-for garden to suit his hectic lifestyle. He wanted a place where he could sit and read the weekend papers, and that could also be a party garden for enjoying with friends.

The existing space was very narrow, covered in concrete (it had been a parking space), with a garage door at one end! Digging up the concrete was not an option, so we built decking over the top instead, and laid natural sandstone alongside as a complement, keeping the angles going across the space to increase the width visually. Three benches and a built-in bar, made of brick and topped with the same timber to make each deck, define the angles still further and make good use of the space.

The planting is sparse and maintenance-free, with just simple bold statements of bamboo, *Fatsia japonica*, *Viburnum davidii*, *Pittosporum tobira* 'Nanum' and grasses like *Stipa arundinacea* – all positioned with aspect in mind. As the garden is used primarily at night, lighting was an important consideration. Little LED spotlights in the decking give a supernatural starry effect, and cheap plastic up-lighters pushed into each container use the foliage to cast ghostly shadows on the walls. A cheap and simple irrigation system concealed under the decking makes watering much less of a chore.

THE RIGHT DESIGN FOR YOU

Garden design, like fashion, comes and goes, and in truth there are very few original ideas around. Most modern designs are interpretations or recycled ideas of 'experiments' by famous designers like Capability Brown, Humphry Repton, Gertrude Jekyll and Luis Barragán, because that's what gardening is: one big experiment. And it's a fickle one at that, giving rise to much heated debate. Ultimately, though, it's your own tastes, personality and the functions you want your garden to fulfil that truly count. You're creating a space for yourself – not for some stuffy design snob to inspect.

Following the latest fashion in gardening is not a good idea because it can stifle your own creativity and, anyway, catwalk gardening is best left where it is – as a spectacle and a bit of razzle-dazzle that provokes a reaction.

GETTING INSPIRATION

People often see the gardens at the Chelsea Flower Show and want to re-create them exactly in their own backyard, without taking into account their lifestyles and the actual space they've got. It's not much good falling in love with a Japanese minimalist garden, with its immaculately raked gravel patterns, if you have a family of tumbling toddlers. Likewise, if you're seldom home, you won't want a large collection of high-maintenance plants – gardening will fast become a chore.

However, it's fun to visit the **gardening shows** where you can tease apart the components of those perfect gardens, and select a few ideas that appeal and might fit your space. For example, you might never have considered using glass as a garden material, yet you now see how effective and striking a glass mulch looks in a contemporary setting. Many of the display gardens at Chelsea have a different function and purpose to the city gardener's backyard; they're designed to be visually appealing, shocking even – alien life-forms from another planet! And they're designed for the judges to see – don't forget that. But do visit as many gardening shows as you can, simply because they're so inspirational, and the experience can be just as thought-provoking and creative when you see what doesn't work in a particular design.

BE CRITICAL

You'll become a knowledgeable critic, too, and all the while you'll absorb ideas and impressions that will be invaluable when you come to plan your own garden. It goes without saying that all of us want a garden to be beautiful, but most of us are looking for something practical as well.

WHICH STYLE?

One of the biggest problems to surmount when you have a small city garden is this: your garden is so small that you feel you can attempt any style – but which one do you choose? I have friends who teeter constantly between a cottage look and a minimalist mini-desert. Sometimes they are reluctant to lose elements of one style and go the whole hog – you can never tell if they're in the process of creating a new garden or destroying the old one.

KEEP IT SIMPLE

To help you here, remember that the smaller the space, the simpler the design should be. That narrows things down a bit. And, also, don't forget you are in total control and, just for once, it's no bad thing to be a control-freak.

Tom Stuart-Smith's design for the Chelsea Flower Show, 2001 – stunning but effortlessly simple

MOOD BOARDS

Create what designers call a mood board – a collection of pictures in magazines or papers that catch your eye. It doesn't matter if they include loads of different gardening styles; just collect as many pictures as you can of the gardens you like, without attempting to categorise them in any way. It doesn't make any difference if they show grand Italian villas or sweeping parkland or flowers in primary colours. When you feel you've chosen enough pictures, pin them to a large piece of hardboard, then step back and see what your collection tells you about the kind of style you'd be happy with for your own garden.

You'll see that the pictures will suggest a direction for your design ideas. In many ways the concept of garden style is an overplayed one, but if you're just starting out, then plumping for just one particular style can be very helpful, and will avoid the dog's dinner look. It does mean that someone else has decided how a garden should look (minimalist, for instance), but you also get a useful set of 'rules' to help you create that look. And in gardening, **rules can easily be broken** if you feel like it. (Sometimes one of the nicest things about gardening is that plants don't have rule books: they have a way of doing their own thing despite our plans, and that's a great point to remember.) So have a look at the various styles and use them as a jumping-off point.

INTERPRETING A STYLE

Your mood board will point towards one style, or perhaps a mixture of two. But it's all a matter of interpretation. Don't slavishly adhere to one particular theme, as in many cases it won't work. Sometimes it seems a gardener 'must have' the garden of his or her dreams above all other factors, and becomes almost obsessed about it. Such gardens can look contrived and uneasy because the style is forced on the space, rather than the space guiding the style. But, of course, if you're in love with a mock Italianate garden, with plastic sculptures in the shadow of the gasworks, go right ahead – **whatever makes you happy**!

Listed below are some of the key garden styles, which should help to anchor your thoughts. You can glean a lot from the principles behind the various styles and combine them sympathetically when designing your own little enclosed Eden. And, it's said, once you've learned the rules, then you can justifiably throw away the rule book.

CLASSIC

With its roots in Greek and Roman times, true classic style is the exact opposite of the cottage garden. The garden is viewed with mathematical precision, where one half of the design usually mirrors the other, be it on the vertical or horizontal axis. Classic style relies on balance, repetition and a true sense of proportion for effect.

DISCIPLINE

There isn't a hair out of place in the truly classical garden; it's a definite set piece and utterly formal. Even unruly plants, positioned to soften the overall effect, are disciplined, with their outlines restricted. Expect to see clean straight lines, lots of squares and rectangles, plenty of clipped box and topiary, and a general restrained sculptural feel. Formal gardens have an **air of repose** – they are quiet places, not really accommodating to small children and footballs. The boundaries might be a manicured yew hedge or a decorative wrought-iron fence. The proportions of classical architecture are much in evidence. In bigger gardens you'll see statues and large urns at the end of a walk or positioned on either side of a bench.

MODERN INTERPRETATION

We tend to think of formal gardens as old-fashioned, but they have enduring design principles that can be brought bang up-to-date. Modern formal gardens use water in rills or geometric pools, and metals like steel and aluminium for garden structures.

COTTAGE GARDEN

Familiar to most of us, the cottage garden is the comfort-food of gardening styles. Pioneered by great designers like William Robinson and Gertrude Jekyll, cottage gardens have a romance that taps into our bucolic back-to-nature fantasies. They are informal, lush, relaxed, overflowing, with scented plants like roses, jasmine or honeysuckle around the door. They have informal borders jam-packed with old-fashioned shrub roses, stuffed with perennials like catmint, pinks and lavenders, along with patches of annual *Godetia*, *Clarkia*, sweet Williams and other favourites from decades ago. Plants self-seed everywhere, and the seedlings are left where they pop up.

The cottage gardener loves plants. They are crammed into the borders wherever there's a space, as design and colour-combining principles fly out of the window in an **orgy of abundance**. The borders may be mixed with shrubs, perennials and bulbs grown all together, or they may be predominantly perennial, dying down in winter. Sometimes vegetables like runner beans or red-leaved beetroot or asparagus are grown among the flowers. Marigolds and love-in-a-mist are everywhere, in between paving cracks, too. And the gardener usually wears an old heirloom sun-hat.

Yes, this is all a bit tongue-in-cheek, but the truth is that many of us are cottage gardeners at heart. Although it is now as clichéd a style as you'll ever wish to see, it's also an enduringly beautiful one, with lots of room for you to be as creative as you wish. The mood of the cottage garden is tranquil and tolerant, its ambience relaxing. Mistakes in this kind of garden are just accepted; perennials are always being moved about. Cottage gardens are labour intensive.

VARIATION ON A THEME

If you apply a little more discipline to this picture, you can have a garden that still echoes the lush carefree mood of the old traditional gardens, but one that is easier to manage. And the new is starting to creep into the cottage garden. Grasses are finding their place as complements in the perennial border and, rather than the old haphazard searching for a space to plonk a new acquisition, borders are designed with the eventual shape and balance of plants in mind.

Cottage gardens suit **people who love plants** and like to tinker in the garden. A lot of city dwellers who have tiny plots hanker for this look but lack the space for the full-blown old-fashioned roses and large perennials that so typify it. However, you can select elements of the style and use them to suggest a cottagey feel: several smaller perennials work well, as do climbing plants. When it comes to building materials, brick and gravel used together, terracotta pots, low picket fences, pebbles and anything worn and weathered suit the cottage-garden style. As you might expect, appropriate garden furniture is usually made of wood or wrought iron.

NATURALISTIC

Naturalistic gardens mimic nature; to the eye they have no real structure at all. Inspiration is taken from the landscape and natural materials, and the effect is **soft, fluid and sinuous**. Boundaries are clothed in plants, and made as inconspicuous as possible.

Although these gardens look effortlessly natural, they have a well thought-out underpinning of design, and this is sometimes more difficult to get right than it is to work with formal shapes. In a sense, you are creating a mini natural environment within the boundary fences or walls, but one that does not particularly link with what lies beyond. A small backyard jungle could fit here, with lush climbers and large-leaved plants filling the space – nature gone wild, the boundary visually obliterated. Or paths could meander through overflowing beds of prairie-style planting in seemingly random patterns. You would expect a pond, much as you might expect to come across one in nature, with no stone edging or formality at all. Instead, the pond merges gradually into the surrounding vegetation and is full of wildlife.

Plants take over in these natural and freeform gardens, and the effect is very relaxing, like a little piece of **wild paradise** transported into your own backyard. You will need a good eye for balance and shape, and how plant forms interrelate, to pull this off successfully. But, as luck would have it, natural gardens are very much in vogue, so it'll be easy to find examples to inspire you.

JAPANESE

This style suits small enclosed city gardens rather well as it utilises clean lines and the careful placement of a small number of features. Japanese gardens are **visually tranquil** and are great for anyone who loves to lounge in peaceful surroundings. They make particular use of texture: think of raked gravel, flat overlapping slates or strategically placed boulders and stones; bamboo, maples and bonsai; beautiful containers; slatted wooden furniture. Combined, these features provide year-round interest The relationships between different shapes and forms, and how they affect each other, are an intrinsic part of Japanese gardens.

BLENDING FORMAL & INFORMAL

Views change as you walk around the Japanese garden, much as you find in woodland gardens with their long winding paths. The planting should be complementary, with flowing informality meeting tightly clipped box, small-leaved *Ligustrum* or rounded clumps of evergreen azaleas. Oriental elements have crept unobtrusively into many contemporary gardens, primarily because of their simplistic style. They appear calm and graceful, but they do need **care and attention**, otherwise the look will become a little frayed at the edges! The key to oriental and Japanese gardens is restraint – it's all too easy to cram in loads of features, only to end up with a right old mess.

MEDITERRANEAN

Mediterranean gardens are the archetype of an outside functional space. They are usually based around a large shaded paved area, where a family can both eat and play, much like a traditional sitting room (but outdoors).

OUTDOOR ROOM

Mediterranean gardens are really **social spaces**; they are not intentional garden designs but rather natural extensions of the home. In colder climates we have taken this hot climate outdoor room and turned it into a style. The Mediterranean style is often thought of as the inspiration for modernist designers who viewed the garden not so much as a horticultural showpiece (like the Victorians and Edwardians), but as a genuine and fully functional room outdoors.

COLOUR & PLANTING

For city gardeners this is a good basis for a backyard, and it doesn't require much maintenance. Expect to see lots of vibrant blues, reds and yellows, which come to the fore in hot sun, and which in colder weather serve to lift the spirits. The walls are usually painted white or in earth tones of orange and brown. The planting is effortlessly natural, with **simple schemes** composed of architectural conifers and evergreens, which grow easily in a hot climate. Terracotta containers also play a big part, especially when planted with lemons, oranges, oleander and lavender.

BE SELECTIVE

In cooler climates it's not a good idea to follow this look to the letter, unless you have a very hot south-facing garden or patio, and plants that thrive under those conditions. You can always select elements of the Mediterranean garden without having the total look. If the focus of your garden is a space for entertaining, then this style is ideal, and it works particularly well in tiny spaces. But if you have a shady north-facing garden, the look will be lost, with even the bright colours appearing dull without direct sunlight.

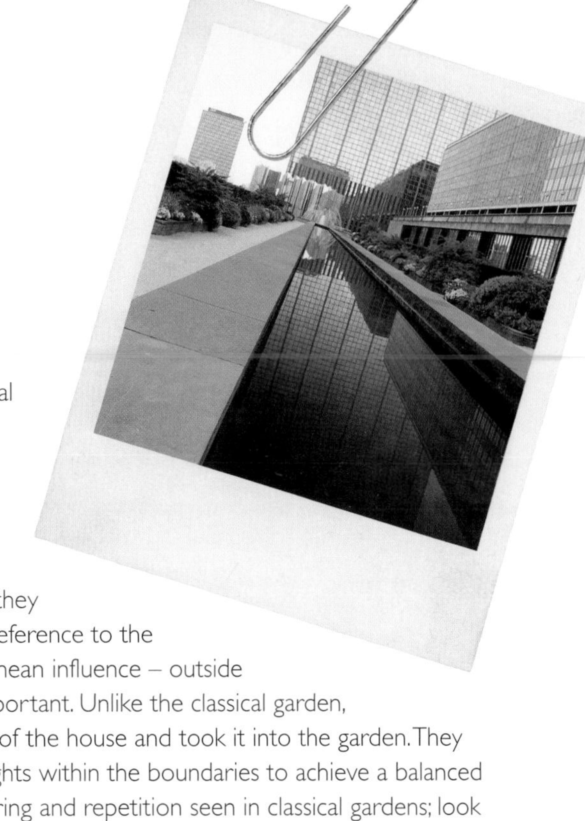

MODERNIST

Until the beginning of the 20th century, the classical formal style was the blueprint for garden designs in this country. But, in the 1920s and '30s, a breakaway movement called the Bauhaus was formed in Germany, and from there it found a home in the US. These innovators wanted to stretch and twist the boundaries of classical style; they used **asymmetrical designs** that made particular reference to the style of the house. They recognised the Mediterranean influence – outside space as an extra room – as being particularly important. Unlike the classical garden, modernist schemes echoed the new architecture of the house and took it into the garden. They used designs and structures of differing visual weights within the boundaries to achieve a balanced look, and left behind the rigid use of formal mirroring and repetition seen in classical gardens; look at Piet Mondrian's paintings and you'll get the idea.

BACK TO BASICS

All non-essentials are stripped away in this look. The key phrase is 'form follows function'. We may not see much in the way of formal gardens in tiny city spaces, but asymmetrical designs are everywhere. The form grows and evolves as new ideas and new times emerge, so you could say a garden designed using asymmetric principles is really up-to-date. If you still want a sense of structure without the rigidity and rule-book symmetry of a truly formal garden, this style is for you.

ARCHITECTURAL CONSIDERATIONS

More than any other, the modernist look demands you carefully consider the character and age of your house, as well as the proportions of windows and doors, so that these dimensions can be incorporated in the garden for the successful integration of both space and house style. This look is very suitable for city gardeners who want outdoor rooms with a strong visual and functional link to the buildings around.

Plants tend to be architectural like *Phormium*, *Cordyline* and *Euphorbia*. Grasses fit in well, too. All are usually planted en masse for effect. Hot tubs, fire pits and plunge pools will add to the look. These gardens combine precision with freedom: you still have **strong design principles** to work from but your own individual interpretation can have a field day.

MINIMALIST

The modern minimalist gardens we often see today, dripping in stainless steel and shiny surfaces, actually have their roots firmly within the modernist style, but they also owe a lot to the restrained simplicity of the Japanese garden. Minimalism is really modernism with most of its clothes off!

LESS IS MORE

While these gardens can be both formal and informal, the overriding principle is 'less is most definitely more'. Expect to see wide expanses of gravel or still water. Planting is usually en masse or in isolation; trees of a single species grouped together, underplanted with ivy or Japanese spurge (*Pachysandra terminalis*). If you want to add another plant to a group, minimalism will frown at you: remember, this is **a look that subtracts as much as it can**, not adds. Colour often plays a big part but it's usually subtle, with various hues of a single colour.

SPACE REQUIREMENTS

Minimalist gardens do need a fair amount of space for the effect to work, otherwise they can appear mean and sterile, as uninviting as a desert. It pays to study the notable designers in this field to see just how they achieved the effects they strived for. These contemporary designs are low maintenance, so they suit busy-busy city folk well.

DECONSTRUCTIVIST

This is the style of garden that causes all the furore every year at the Chelsea Flower Show. 'Is *that* a garden?', you might well overhear, voiced in disbelief.

WHERE ARE THE PLANTS?

Well, these gardens do challenge all the cherished notions of what a garden should be, so these designs are not for everyone. If you like plants, you will find they are secondary to the design, or even, it might seem, forgotten altogether. If you think modernist gardens are beyond the pale, these exemplars of chaos theory will have you running for cover!

Abandoning all the rules might seem a fun idea, but basic garden principles still need to be understood before you go mad and throw away the rule book completely. I like to think of these designs as **playthings for designers** who like to challenge themselves to come up with something shocking and new to set us all talking.

These designs are ultra-contemporary, and may be made of sharp angular forms, or a mixture of angles and curves; again, balance is important, as is the ability to 'read' the design accurately for success. Expect cutting-edge materials like glass, metal, plastic, as well as water used in glittering pools or even, as one Chelsea garden featured, running uphill.

LIMITED LIFESPAN

The novelty value of deconstructivist gardens can wear thin, however, if you are living with them all the time. Plus you'll find that they'll date pretty quickly – much the same as ripped, snow-washed denim really...

Deconstructivist gardens aren't actually a style in their own right; most are hybrids utilising the principles of other garden styles and, like a teenager in a strop, **breaking the rules** just for the hell of it: think of Andy Warhol's baked bean tins, works by Damien Hirst, or any entries for the Turner Prize!

THE PROFESSIONALS

fig:6.0 crane

CREATE A VISUAL LINK BETWEEN THE HOUSE AND THE GARDEN

CONSIDERING YOUR HOME

With small outdoor spaces, it's important to think of your house and garden together, rather than as completely separate units. This is how modernist designers, in particular, begin their plans. In order to understand how to forge a link between the two units, you actually need to look closely at your house and forget the garden for a while.

FORGING LINKS

Take the indoors first, and make notes about the colours you have used on the walls, the style of furniture you prefer, be it modern or traditional in appearance. (This is a bit like a written mood board of what you already have.) You should consider paintings and ornaments, too. All these are indications of your personality, and you want to carry that **expression of your taste** out into the garden if you can. There are instances when you may feel you want a complete change of scene and see the garden as your alter ego, where you can express a part of yourself that you haven't expressed inside the house. If this is what you want to do and it gives you pleasure, then go for it, but with conviction. For home owners and gardeners who want to use their skill and have fun in making the whole of their property knit together in a related way, think of echoing your tastes from the house interior into the garden. This has the plus side of actually making your property feel bigger.

Many of us want to give the impression that the house does indeed extend into the garden, so take a good **look at the outside of your house**, its style and the materials from which it's made. If your house is built from yellow London stocks, for example, what could be nicer and give a more natural continuity than to use bricks of a similar colour in any new freestanding walls? And why not run the terracotta flooring tiles from the kitchen out of the back door and onto the patio? In this way you forge a link between the inside and outside.

DESIGN PRINCIPLES

We've had a look at styles of gardening, but within all the different types there are basic principles of good design that can be terribly confusing for beginner and fanatic (me) alike. A few obvious principles make useful pointers to bear in mind when you are planning: use them as a checklist, if you like.

SIMPLICITY

In city gardens, simplicity is king. You have to accept you just can't grow everything, let alone have every feature you desire, because the effect will be more dog's dinner than peaceful paradise! I know it's hard, especially when you've formulated a list as long as your arm, but exercising controlled restraint over your creativity is something you will be able to congratulate yourself on. Making a garden design look brilliantly **simple and elegant** is the sure sign of a gardener who has earned his/her spurs, and makes you far more aware of all the slipshod design around you.

Show moderation and avoid plastering the garden with too many different features, materials or plants; it'll look fussy, haphazard and unplanned. Builders' catalogues are packed full of different paving slabs, timber setts and slate tiles, all of which are appealing in their own right, but it's wise to use just a few. Depending upon the style of the house, I find that a maximum of three or four different types of materials is usually enough; gravel, timber decking, sandstone of a similar colour and copper would do nicely, but any more and you'll become visually disturbed! There's nothing wrong with an eclectic mix of materials – just make sure the transition from one to another is

smooth so the garden keeps a sense of harmony.

HARMONY

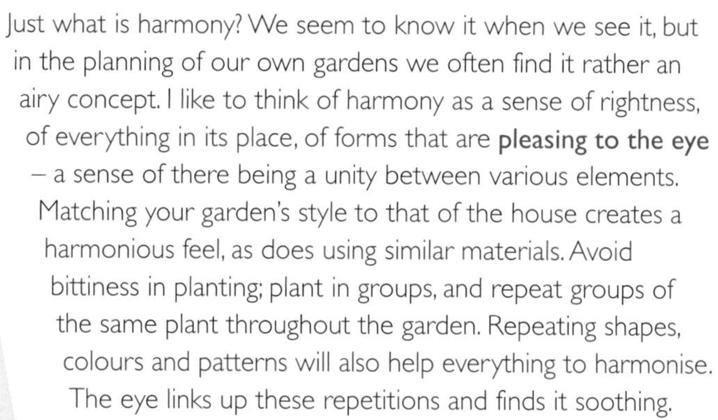

Just what is harmony? We seem to know it when we see it, but in the planning of our own gardens we often find it rather an airy concept. I like to think of harmony as a sense of rightness, of everything in its place, of forms that are **pleasing to the eye** – a sense of there being a unity between various elements. Matching your garden's style to that of the house creates a harmonious feel, as does using similar materials. Avoid bittiness in planting; plant in groups, and repeat groups of the same plant throughout the garden. Repeating shapes, colours and patterns will also help everything to harmonise. The eye links up these repetitions and finds it soothing.

PROPORTION & SCALE

We've all seen plants that are too big for their allotted space – the tree that dominates a garden so that nothing else will grow and just looks so enormous; a tiny pond or small flower bed in the middle of a vast lawn, where it looks sad and insignificant and loses all impact. If you have a small house, curb your ambitions to go big in the garden! Check on the ultimate sizes of plants so they won't turn into monsters. Make your paths wide enough for two to walk in comfort, but not so big that they dwarf your beds and borders. Designing an oversized lawn or patio to trick the eye into thinking the space is bigger may, in fact, have the opposite effect. It won't be in proportion as there isn't any space left for planting.

Paving materials must be sympathetic to the overall size of the garden. Large Yorkstone flags in a small garden will make it appear smaller, whereas small granite setts might be a better choice. You can always combine the two – just try to find a **happy medium** and make sure everything relates well together. It takes only one oversized tree, pergola, path, patio or water feature to make a garden feel smaller. Related to proportion is balance…

BALANCE

Balance is concerned with the effects achieved by different masses and voids (empty spaces) in the garden, and their relationship to each other. For example, avoid planting all the evergreens in one area of the garden and leaving the deciduous shrubs and herbaceous borders at the other end; in winter the effect will be too heavy at the evergreen end and too light at the other. For a balanced effect, thread the evergreens through the whole scheme.

Grouping all your tall plants together on one side of the garden may also look unbalanced. In this kind of design, you would need a large area of lawn to act as a counterweight. An example of balanced planting would be a large fluffy-headed tree opposed by a much smaller but denser collection of evergreens.

Remember that when a new garden is started, it won't look as balanced as you'd like it to because maturity, along with the parallel growth in size/mass, takes time to achieve.

Achieving balance with colour is an **enjoyable challenge** with which all gardeners wrestle. Not only do you have to consider the colours that look 'right' next to each other, but you also have to think of the way that plants look at different times of the year. Think about when the flowers fade and only foliage is left. Consider what colour the leaves will turn in autumn. And to complicate matters still further, what are the plants going to look like in winter? Think of the shape and form of deciduous trees and shrubs when they are stripped of all their leaves.

Ian's garden, Newcastle

MOVEMENT

What is movement when applied to a garden? It doesn't just mean plants (like bamboo) that move in the wind, or obvious waterfalls and fountains. Rather, it is the eye and your body that move and are encouraged to travel around the garden from one point of interest to another. Creating movement in a garden is essential, otherwise it may appear static and more like a two-dimensional picture than an inviting space. And in all but the smallest of gardens it's **easily achievable**.

The careful positioning of focal points and the use of height help to create this sense of movement. For example, tall hedges that border a narrow path urge you to walk along that path because you sense there's more to see beyond it, and your curiosity is aroused. You might position a small statue, or an urn brimming with lilies, at the end of a path to invite you to go towards it. A wooden pergola hanging with wisteria, or a small steel tunnel laced with laburnum, work in a similar way, linking static and more tranquil areas of the garden.

The way paving materials are used can have a dramatic affect, making spaces quiet or more dynamic. Grass, gravel and crazy paving are considered static in themselves, unless they form a sweeping shape that tapers at the end; this is the **clever use of false perspective** that appears to make a space longer. Static materials are ideal for seating areas where a sense of movement is unnecessary and could make lounge-lizards and diners feel a little restless.

Brick paving laid in a diagonal pattern or 'running bond' has a strong sense of forward movement, and is great for paths that curve out of sight; you want to go on and seek the mystery (or reward) at the end. Heavy wooden sleepers placed across a gravel path encourage you to walk more slowly and consider the garden on either side. (This is a neat trick if you want people to stop and look at those prize plant specimens you've strategically positioned either side.) On the other hand, if you align the sleepers longitudinally, you'll find yourself skipping on through.

INTEREST

It may seem obvious but interest is really what it's all about when you design your garden. You're painting a 3-D picture for you and your family to enjoy. By blindly adhering to design principles, you could end up with a garden that has no appeal for you. Design tends to depersonalise, and what makes the garden interesting to you is the **personal touch** – always. Choice is the major tool at your disposal: choice of shape, form, colour and texture, all of which can be reflected in hard and soft landscaping.

And what about the plants? Even if you forget colour, just look at the different shapes and textures. Plants can be prostrate, rounded, upright, weeping, conical, spreading, fastigiate, erect, mat-forming, mound-forming, clump-forming or climbing – phew! Their leaves can be prickly, spiny, woolly, waxy, ribbed, corrugated, shiny, matt, glaucous, warty, hard or soft. Their flowers can be nodding, erect, pendent, horizontal, pea-like, tubular, saucer-shaped; they can be on their own, in clusters, spikes, umbels and racemes, to name but a few formations.

So take a close look at all these categories and see what grabs your attention, what draws your eye. When it comes to plants, there's so much to play with and so many different combinations to try, that now's the time to start playing around with them and **having some fun**.

SURPRISE, SURPRISE!

Pranks and party tricks in the garden? Well, not quite, though these elements can be incorporated, even as temporary features, such as lanterns and seasonal lights.

No garden is complete without an element of surprise; it adds a lively mischief to the garden and it will **make your visitors smile**. One of the most successful tricks is creating different rooms within the garden, each with a different character. Use vertical partitions like walls, pergolas and hedges to create secret areas in the garden that stay hidden from sight until you turn the corner. A series of focal points, like sculptures or architectural plants, are all surprise elements, too. Some sculptures can be half-hidden; I once saw a small collection of garden gnomes peeping out from beneath the low canopy of a maple, and they almost made me jump!

Unusual lighting, like underwater lights shining onto a wall of water, will bring out the 'Ohh!' factor. Lining paths with subtle solar lights that lead to a sculpture lit from below by an uplighter will create the atmosphere of an event about to happen.

Deception and illusion are more sneaky ways to create surprise. Very small courtyard gardens can pull this off superbly by using **mirrors** to create the illusion of a doorway into another garden. 'Trompe l'oeil' uses painted trellis and the trick of perspective to give the impression that there's more to the garden than there really is. Think surprise, think secret. The discovery of something that's not where you'd expect to find it always evokes the child in us. This is where your personality can have free rein. Who knows, the practical joker's garden might be the next 'big thing'...

Leicester

Decking is well within the scope of the amateur gardener

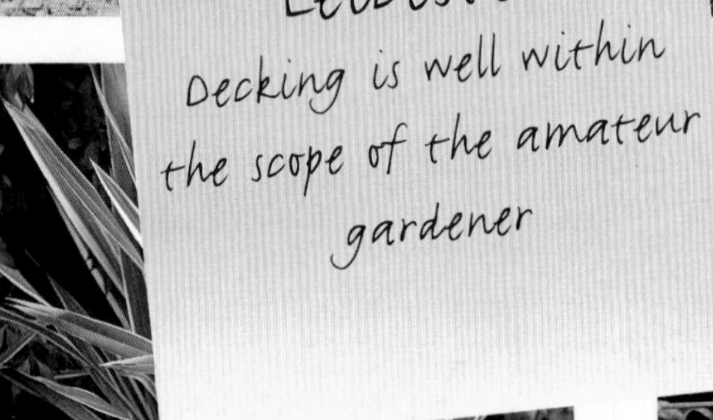

All gardens need somewhere peaceful to chill out in

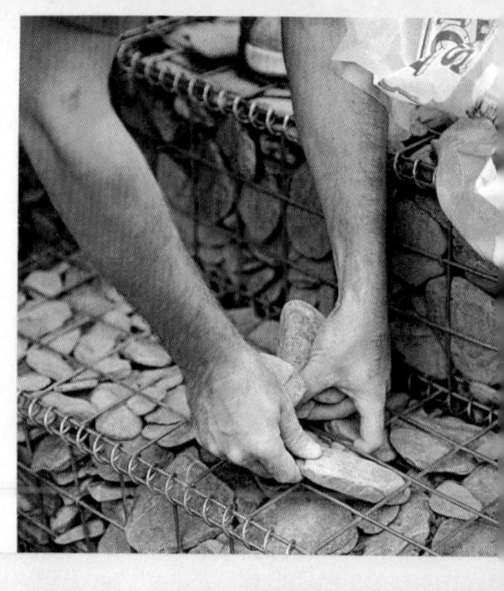

Don't forget to
orientate your design
so that it looks good
from the house

LEICESTER

Bhavana and Nigel's very long narrow garden presented two big problems: the soil was thick clay, and the bottom half of the garden was like a high 'terrace', where builders had dumped soil when digging foundations for an extension. The house itself was tastefully contemporary, with classic elements, and the couple wanted to continue this ordered simplicity outside.

Instead of building a brick wall, which would have been expensive and time-consuming, I decided to use steel gabions (slate-filled wire containers) to retain the pile of soil and to make the steps. I then created a secluded decked area, hidden by bamboo screening and *Fargesia nitida* 'Nymphenburg', at the back of the garden. Here, Bhavana practises yoga or simply enjoys some peace and quiet.

The planting had to be robust because of the soil, so among shrubs like *Amelanchier lamarckii*, *Philadelphus* 'Belle Etoile', *Viburnum* x *burkwoodii*, *Berberis thunbergii* 'Atropurpurea Nana', *Euphorbia characias* subsp. *wulfenii* and *Phormium tenax*, I planted lots of tough evergreen groundcover like *Pachysandra terminalis*, ivy, *Tiarella wherryii* and *Pleioblastus pygmaeus*. Two large birch trees act as focal points, especially at night when lights placed at their base accentuate the colour of the bark.

The specially fabricated steel pond and candlesticks act as simple focal points, adding a touch of modern-day elegance to the design.

GETTING STUCK IN

Once you have a few ideas about the style of garden you'd like, it's time to start thinking about a design. Keep your list of wants and needs to hand, and try to include as many of them in your design as is realistically possible, so that everyone who uses the garden will be satisfied with the outcome.

Measure your space accurately – a cheap retractable reel tape measure is perfect for the job. Note the exact position of your house in relation to the garden, especially the doors and windows, and mark these on the plan. You'll need to orientate the design so that the view of the garden from the house is a good one.

To get an idea of whether the features that you'd like will actually fit in your garden, it's worth using your measurements to draw a scale plan. I'm not talking about some over-elaborate watercolour here, just a simple pencil drawing that'll help you not only visualise your space more easily, but also be useful when it comes to ordering materials.

For my scale plans, I use large A1 sheets of graph paper, which you can buy at any good art shop; there are also garden design computer programs available, although I'm a fan of doing it by hand – it feels a bit more creative. For a scale plan, you'll need a scale rule. Most have more than one scale on the side so, regardless of the actual size of your garden, you'll be able to fit it onto a piece of paper.

KEEP IT SIMPLE

Once you've drawn the outline of your garden to scale, mark in the position of those existing features that you want to retain: I don't mean just the large trees and shrubs, but also the garden shed, greenhouse and any existing paths or walls. Note down the position of things you want to screen and parts of the garden that need to be made more private. Then mark where you want essential features like the bins and washing line to go. Place them within easy reach of the house, though; in bad weather you'll want to access them quickly, and it is easy to disguise them with trellis, willow fencing or tall grasses.

You're now ready to work out where the new features should go: the patio, the lawn and play areas, for example. If you're a novice at garden design, geometric shapes are the simplest to work with. They have an inherent balance and can be grouped together easily or overlapped to produce an infinite number of ground shapes, both formal and informal.

... AND FUN

Grab some spare cardboard, cut out various shapes to the same scale as the garden, each piece representing a particular feature, and move them around on your plan to see where they look best. Look at the gaps between them and the edge as areas for planting. Make it fun and creative. On your plan draw where you'd like to have those private/secluded areas, too.

Doing this is easier than you think... Imagine your garden is the size of this page. Cut out three squares of coloured paper to the same scale as the garden, and place them on the page, overlapping each other at the corners. Note where due south is, so that you don't plan your sunbathing area in dense shade, then just try out different combinations. The first square could be a patio, bordered by flowering shrubs and herbaceous perennials; the second a lawn, edged in box topiary, again surrounded by planting. The third square could be a vegetable patch, screened by a willow 'fedge' (fence-cum-hedge). A small circle next to the lawn could make a private seating area under the canopy of a silver birch you've decided to keep. Try everything at different angles on the plan; just keep moving the shapes around until it feels right.

HOW TO USE A SCALE RULE

Some people find a scale rule scary, but the principle is simple. On the side, you'll find markings for different scales: 1:20, 1:50, 1:100, and so on. The first number means 1 centimetre, the second number, say, 50, means 50 centimetres. So, at a scale of 1:50, one centimetre on paper counts as half a metre on the ground. At this scale, a garden 5m square would end up measuring 10cm square on paper. When you start to position the features you want in your new garden, you simply size them to the same scale. Just keep rechecking your measurements, and ensure that you're still using the same scale.

Working out what you want and where is a fun task, but it takes time and patience. Expect your ideas to change as you look at gardening books. When I'm designing a garden, I think of this part of the process as a simple jigsaw puzzle. I play around with different shapes for hours, sometimes days. There is no right solution for your garden, just many possibilities. But something will gel along the way and... Eureka! You have the beginnings of a garden. Keep all your grand designs simple and, as you grow in confidence, you can add more features as the fancy takes you.

GET DOODLING

I have to be fair: there are some of us who hate the idea of graphs and shunting tiny pieces of paper around – it just doesn't seem real. If you're struggling to visualise your garden on paper, take a spray can of non-toxic paint, or fill an empty lemonade bottle with soft dry sand, and use your garden as a life-size doodle pad. Mark out your design with the proposed positions of hedges, arbours, flowerbeds and seating areas directly on the ground. This is a good way of designing 'grass roots' style. And it's easy to scuff it out and start all over again. Doing it this way helps you to check the proportions of features against each other and the garden as a whole, which is sometimes difficult to visualise on paper. Nothing is set in stone, so there's no need to feel intimidated. Enjoy experimenting and debating with the family about what looks best.

A common mistake is to plan the patio smaller than you actually need it. I find that it's useful to draw the shape of the table on the ground, and actually put garden chairs round it. Move the chairs in and out to check that there is enough room for people to sit comfortably at the table. You might find that this results in another feature, like the lawn, having to disappear completely.

KEEP MAINTENANCE IN MIND

During the planning process, remember that you will have to maintain whatever you design. How much work do you really want to do? Cutting hedges, mowing lawns and trimming edges are all tasks that need to be done on a regular basis; in summer, a lawn might need mowing once or even twice a week. Will your design make it needlessly difficult to cut the grass? I've seen a garden design with a lawn that rolled right up to the edge of a water-filled steel rill. It looked beautiful, but I couldn't help wondering how you could trim the edges of the grass without the clippings falling into the water and then blocking the pump.

A garden must be planned so that the maintenance is easy, and this is one reason why it's sometimes best not to have a lawn in a small town garden – you might be better off paving the whole thing instead. Don't plump for something simply to wow your friends if it means that you have to look after it 24/7. Gardens are places for relaxing – remember?

THE LIMITS OF DIY

The easiest way to keep costs down is to do all the work yourself. But don't aim too high; like everyone, you'll have limits when it comes to do-it-yourself. Unless you can bribe friends in the building trade, you may need to call on **professional help**. Contractors will be needed for more ambitious projects or to build specialist features like retaining walls. If you are planning lots of lighting, you may need to factor in the price of an electrician as well, unless, of course, it's a low-voltage set and you can do it yourself. If you recognise the need for a specialist contractor, just make sure you get loads of quotes – the price of the simplest job can vary dramatically.

THE SKELETON

Paths, paving, walls, fences and steps all make up the skeleton of a design. They form the core structure of a garden, holding all the other elements together, and they have an important aesthetic, as well as practical, role. Try not to view the hard landscaping in isolation, though; it's just one part of the bigger picture. Keep in mind the garden's living framework: the trees, evergreen shrubs and hedges, all of which will impact on the style of your garden.

PLACES TO GO, PEOPLE TO SEE

Many garden centres now sell a wide range of paving materials, timber constructions and fencing. Don't buy without first checking out large DIY stores; although their range is often limited, it's usually a lot cheaper. For large quantities, try a builder's merchant or timber yard; they buy in bulk, passing the saving onto you. If you're spending a lot, always **press for a discount**, or at the very least free delivery; you may be refused, but there is no harm in asking.

For rustic, weathered and old materials, check out your local reclamation yard. They're a goldmine, stocking tons of stuff, including old chimney pots, reclaimed York stone, wrought-iron gates and weather-beaten wheelbarrows – all perfect for eclectic, cottagey designs. Don't expect them to be particularly cheap, though, but you can haggle and, with luck, you might pick up a bargain.

Contemporary materials like metal and plastic aren't commonly available, and can easily cost a fortune so, again, make sure you **shop around** to save money.

A PATIO SHOULD BE BOTH GOOD LOOKING AND HARD WEARING

THE PATIO

Patios are usually the main focus of small city gardens, and must be able to take a lot of wear and tear: the kids play on them, chairs get dragged across them, pots are moved about on them and, in some cases, you get motorbike maintenance performed on them! Ideally, your patio should be constructed of a really solid material. Gravel or bark are cheap, but they really aren't up to the job; you don't want a material that's going to shift about, become waterlogged or sprout weeds.

Try to site your patio in a position where it gets the most sun for those times when you usually enjoy your garden – it's pointless having an expensive and well-designed seating area that only gets the sun while you're out at work. Why not build more than one patio, the second in a secluded spot where you can catch the last of the late-afternoon sunshine when you get home from work?

If the garden is really tiny, it is better to pave the whole thing using a combination of materials. Take your cue from your house and surroundings. If the walls are brick, then perhaps opt for the same or, at the very least, use sympathetic materials that will blend in.

The following are some of the more readily available materials that can be used to make a garden patio. All of them have functional as well as aesthetic qualities. Although tarmac and concrete are undeniably useful surfacing materials and particularly hardwearing, they're ugly and monotonous, making them poor choices for the small city garden.

SANDSTONE

Natural sandstone, or York stone as it's also commonly known, is a superb paving material, ideal for patios and paths. But it is pricey! Being a natural material, it has a lovely texture to it and comes in various shadings that change colour when it rains. To give an aged, established look to your patio, this has to be one of your first choices. Use different-sized slabs for a relaxing random effect, or just one size for a more dramatic uniform look. As with all slab-laying, think carefully about their position before you bed them down in concrete. Try the pattern out on the ground beforehand. With York stone, you need to watch out for algae; in prolonged damp weather this can easily end up making the slabs slippery, so use a stiff broom or pressure sprayer to remove it.

BRICK

Bricks are traditionally the favoured paving material for cottage and courtyard gardens because they provide such a wonderful link to the house. They're also so versatile that they work well with almost any other material. They come in **any colour or finish** you can imagine, from glazed ceramic bricks to rustic yellow stocks. All are easy to lay, though it's time-consuming work. The most important factor to consider, apart from appearance, is that the bricks should be frost-proof and durable. Choose the finish carefully as very smooth bricks can become slippery in the wet.

Cheaper than bricks are imitation brick pavers made of concrete. Admittedly, these have their uses, in driveways especially, but for intimate settings like a city garden, their monotonous colour and texture don't work so well, and they will always look like a cheap cousin to the real thing. It's also very difficult to find other materials that complement them.

GRANITE

Granite is a tough, streetwise paving material and is commonly pink, grey, brown or black in colour. You can buy it sawn into slabs, but it is amazingly expensive this way. So, it's usually sold as setts: small rectangular pieces of granite about the size of a brick; half-setts are half-brick-size. Granite setts have a rough uneven surface; for **texture appeal**, they score one hundred per cent! For paths they give good grip, but for large seating areas you may prefer something smoother. Unlike big paving slabs, setts are easy to handle, simple to lay and, because of their small size, work wonderfully in curved patterns, circles or fans. Granite setts complement natural stone beautifully, and are ideal as edging for gravelled areas. Use them for giving interesting detail to monotonous concrete drives.

TERRACOTTA, SLATE & MARBLE TILES

Tiles are tricky things to lay, requiring a smooth hard concrete base. They can appear very busy and restless unless they're used in regimented patterns. 'Crazy paving' is a definite no-no! Marble is expensive, best left to wealthy people with inspired classical schemes. Choose terracotta or slate if you're on a tight budget. In Mediterranean and Moorish designs, use terracotta tiles in intimate corners to complete the look; their **reflective qualities** will enliven the shadiest spot, although they can become slippery when wet or even (horror of horrors!) too hot to walk on barefoot in full sun.

Slate tiles not only come in many shades of grey to green, and even plum, but they can also be cut into strips and embedded on edge to make intricate swirling patterns, which look amazing. But don't attempt to do an entire patio this way; it will be uncomfortable to walk on barefoot and take ages to do, not to mention costing a fortune.

BRICKWORK PATTERNS

There are numerous traditional patterns, or 'bonds', for laying bricks. Choose the right bond and you can manipulate both perspective and movement.

Stretcher bond Makes a path appear wider.

Herringbone or diagonal herringbone A running bond like herringbone creates a strong sense of movement and makes a path look longer. Use it in long flowing curves to lead the eye on through an area.

Basketweave A static bond like basketweave is easy on the eye and perfect for patios and relaxation areas.

CONCRETE PAVING

Concrete slabs are the cheapest paving material you can buy; most garden centres and builders merchants stock a wide range in different finishes, shapes and sizes, some of which look just like natural stone. If you like brick paving but haven't the patience to lay individual units, you can buy imitation slabs that are imprinted with a herringbone pattern to look just like bricks; this way you can lay eight 'bricks' at a time. Some even look just like terracotta tiles.

Concrete slabs are ideal for both patios and paths, especially if you opt for those with a rough surface texture. Avoid brightly coloured slabs, though, as they don't weather well, let alone harmonise with planting or brickwork. If you want the concrete paving to retire into the background, stick to slabs in neutral shades of grey; these complement almost anything. Lay them in a simple grid pattern, or lay rectangular slabs in a staggered bond across a space to give the illusion of width.

DECKING

We've all taken to decking in a big way and although some think it's now a cliché, I have to disagree. When is a natural material ever a cliché?

Decking can be constructed from either hardwood or softwood. Hardwood is more expensive, yet it won't need much maintenance. Softwood needs to be treated with a non-toxic preservative before and after you've created your deck. Most timber merchants will sell both, treated or untreated. Decking comes in planks or ready-made squares that can be stained, laid in different patterns or contoured to fit around tree trunks. Because it can be cut to almost any shape, decking can be used anywhere: extended out over ponds, on roof terraces, to form boardwalks through woodland planting. Instead of building the typical square or rectangular deck, why not construct a free-form shape and have it meander out into the garden?

If your garden slopes, decking is ideal; you can provide level 'stepping stones' from one part of the garden to another, offering new perspectives. If you have a concrete yard and loathe the idea of digging it all up, simply use decking to cover it; it's perfect for the job.

Decking is well within the scope of the amateur carpenter, too. You just need a substantial framework, usually made of 4 x 2in pre-treated timber, which is mounted on sturdy posts embedded in concrete; this keeps the deck off the ground and prevents it from rotting. The deck boards are then nailed or screwed across this frame. You can create a strong sense of direction by positioning the boards to contrast with your surroundings.

TIMBER SETTS & LOG SLICES

These make beautiful floors for seating areas in naturalistic settings. They obviously don't last as long as York stone, so are best used in secluded spots throughout the garden, not as the main patio.

Hardwood slices last longer, but treated softwood is a lot cheaper. For a paved area, simply choose sections that are at least 150mm (6in) thick, and lay them directly onto soil that has been excavated and then compacted to the appropriate depth. Butt them up as close as possible, and fill in the gaps with gravel or bark chippings. To prevent them moving around, secure pre-treated timber planks or sunken railway sleepers around the edge.

Larger slices can be used as stepping stones down a bark-covered path. Under trees, these can get very slippery, so staple chicken wire to the tops. Logs laid horizontally can also be used to make cheap steps, but they must be firmly pegged into position with either steel rods or wooden stakes.

TIMBER SLEEPERS

These heavyweights of patio flooring have a solid and rustic feel that complements both cottage gardens and contemporary settings. Dominant features in their own right, they require you to have an awareness of proportions and balance with regard to surrounding features; large plants or lush planting are needed to offset their size. Avoid old railway sleepers, though. They're uneven, which makes them an unsuitable surface for tables and chairs, and they're also contaminated with oil, which in hot weather will stain your clothes. For seating areas, always buy new hardwood sleepers, even though they are a little bit more expensive. Sleepers also make great raised beds, which can double up as seating – or steps, in the right setting.

You won't need a foundation to lay timber sleepers; they're heavy enough to cope on their own. Just compact and level the soil underneath. And you won't need to incorporate a slope into the patio either, since rainwater will drain away between the gaps.

HOW TO LAY A SIMPLE PATIO

It's very important to give your patio a good foundation in life, so sit it on a firm base. The standard sub-base for most paving is 75–100mm (3–4in) of well-compacted crushed hardcore or stone. A substantial sub-base is important to prevent subsidence, especially on heavy soils that move according to whether they're wet or dry.

• If you're laying slabs, dig out the soil deep enough to accommodate the depth of the slab (say, 40mm/1½in), the depth of the foundation (say, 100mm/4in), and a further 50mm (2in) for the bedding material or mortar. Save the topsoil you dig out for use elsewhere in the garden.

• Compact your sub-base well. Get a mechanical vibrating plate from your hire shop – it's a simple machine to use, and the guys dropping it off will start it up and show you what to do. For hard-to-reach places, use the top of a sledgehammer.

• Continually recheck the depth you're digging out, using a spirit level on a long straight edge to make sure it's reasonably flat.

• Fill in and compact any low spots to make a level base for the paving.

• If you're laying small paving units like bricks, you will need restraints, usually made of timber, positioned around the edge to hold it all in place. Position the top of the restraints at the same height as you want your paving to finish, and secure them with permanent timber or metal pegs before filling the excavated area with your sub-base.

• If you have a gentle slope, the best way to level this off for a patio is to 'cut and fill'. Cut out the higher part of the slope, then use the dug-out material to fill in the lower part. Take care if you're doing this on a steep gradient, as you'll need retaining walls at the lower end. You'll probably need professional help for this since the walls will have to withstand a large amount of pressure.

LAYING PAVING

The usual mix for laying York stone, granite, pre-cast concrete and brick paving consists of six parts sharp sand and one part ordinary Portland cement. Mix thoroughly before adding any water. After you've added the water, the mix should be an even colour and damp enough so that it's easily worked with a bricklaying trowel or shovel. Take care not to add too much water all in one go, otherwise you'll end up with an awful sloppy mess.

Paving slabs are laid in one of two ways: the 'five-spot' method or the 'mortar-bed' method (see below). Whichever method you choose, hire an angle grinder to cut the slabs so that they fit snugly around drains and manhole covers.

Concrete paving slabs are butted up to one another, meaning that there are no gaps between them. Natural stone, including imitation stone, is usually laid with a 5–10mm (¼–½in) gap between each one, which is then pointed with a 6:1 mixture of dry soft sand and cement. Brush the mix over the top with a soft broom, and then use a small section of hosepipe to firm it into each joint and to smooth it off level. Make sure that it's unlikely to rain when you do this job, or the 'pointing' mix will stain your paving. Alternatively, the joints can be filled with contrasting gravel; you can also use sifted topsoil, which will encourage mosses and lichens to grow through, but I find that weeds have a habit of infiltrating these cracks extremely fast.

Aim for a flat and reasonably level surface, but with a gentle slope away from the house so that any water doesn't puddle or, more importantly, compromise the damp-proof course (DPC) – look for a layer of black membrane or a line of dark blue-coloured bricks or slate at the base of the house walls. Patio edges, paths, stonework, etc., should ideally be two courses of bricks (approximately 150mm/6in) lower than the DPC, so you don't get rising damp in your home.

In most cases, you can direct any run-off water into flowerbeds or onto the lawn, but in small courtyard gardens or sunken gardens you might find that it's necessary to get a drainage system installed beforehand.

If you're laying a substantial amount of paving, get a professional landscaping firm to do it for you; I often do! Areas of hard standing, especially those next to houses, need to be built properly if you want to avoid expensive complications in the future.

Definitely get some professional help to lay a driveway, especially if you intend to use imitation bricks made out of concrete. Laying them properly is quite difficult; they need to be butt-jointed together on a compacted layer of sharp sand, and then compacted again with a vibrating plate. As well as being tricky to do, the sheer monotony of it all will bore you to tears!

LAYING PAVING SLABS

Paving slabs are laid using either the 'five-spot' method or the 'mortar-bed' method. Five-spotting involves applying five dollops of mortar (5:1 soft sand:cement) to the ground where the slab is to be laid (one spot for the middle, and one for each corner), and then tapping down on the slab gently. Although it's easier to get the slab in position this way, I prefer the mortar-bed method because the whole slab is supported and less likely to move. Spread a 50mm (2in) bed of mortar (5:1 sharp sand: cement) over your hardcore base and use a trowel to create some furrows, so the mortar has somewhere to go when you tamp down the slab with a rubber hammer. Use a spirit level across each slab, and across the adjoining ones, to make sure they're all level.

A TAPERING PATH WILL MAKE YOUR GARDEN APPEAR LONGER

FROM A TO B

Paths are not only a way of getting from one area of the garden to another, they're also an integral part of a garden's backbone that will, if positioned correctly, give it structure like no other feature. Their style will affect the whole atmosphere of a garden, so consider their make-up and orientation carefully. Paths that stretch down a garden will make it appear longer, especially if you manipulate perspective and taper the path as it goes away from you. Paths that sweep across a garden will make it feel wider. Mark out your paths with a spray can of non-toxic paint, and play around with different shapes; you'll be amazed how a simple **change in direction** will affect your space.

Main paths should be wide enough to allow two people to walk comfortably along side by side; secondary paths need be wide enough only to accommodate the width of a wheelbarrow or dustbin.

Many of the materials used for patios and seating areas can also be made into paths. Doing this consciously can **provide continuity** from one area to the next. Paths also help define and segregate different styles in a garden with different 'rooms'.

Whereas patios should be constructed of a durable stable material, paths can be constructed of almost anything, even loose materials like cobbles, gravel or chipped bark, all of which are reasonably cheap – ideal if you need to spend most of your budget on a seating area, the nucleus of any garden. Materials needn't be used in isolation, however. Some of the most **attractive paths** combine solid and loose materials in juxtaposition: granite setts bordered by sleepers, or brick squares with gravel infill. Despite the ease of mixing materials in paths, keep things simple. Over-complication, using many different materials in complex patterns, will make a small garden look fussy.

PEBBLES & COBBLES

Pebbles and cobbles are sourced from riverbeds and beaches the world over. As such, they are available in many different colours and patterns, from white through to oranges, blues through to black. They can be laid loose, or you can pack them tightly into a bed of mortar to create intricate patterns, especially when you use **different colours and sizes**. Either way they provide an interesting contrast to both planting and smooth surfaces like natural stone.

You can pile them next to a meandering path, or fill little pockets amongst randomly laid natural stone – a lovely juxtaposition of texture. They work wonderfully with enormous boulders, which can be used as focal points, the smaller cobbles and pebbles tailing off underneath as though they've recently been unearthed. Smaller boulders can also be laid as an attractive and sympathetic edge to a path. For a beach effect, simply form a bank of cobbles along the edge of an informal pool.

BARK CHIPPINGS

In a natural setting, bark makes a wonderful path, but it fits practically anywhere, in cottage and contemporary designs alike. Best of all, bark chippings are cheap. The thicker landscaping grades are surprisingly durable, and look great when allowed to run seamlessly into adjacent planting. They make a safe and soft surface for children's play areas. Blackbirds will always be tossing the chippings aside as they search for grubs, and some bulbs will love to fight their way through it. Avoid the fine-grade chippings sold as a surface mulch for repressing weeds and retaining soil moisture; they rot down too quickly to be used for paths.

GRAVEL

Of all the inorganic surface materials, gravel is the **cheapest and easiest** one to lay. Like all loose materials, it's ideal for bumpy ground as it self-levels and can be raked smooth as and when needed. Choose colours that complement surrounding paving or brickwork. If you don't, it's surprisingly easy to end up with something garish, even when used in contemporary settings. Use light-coloured gravel or, better still, glass gravel, to brighten up shady gardens. For a really informal look, plant large alpines

and herbaceous perennials within it to break up the mass. Alternatively, use it as a foil for bold structural planting in minimalist designs. Gravel is great for the security-conscious as it has a reassuringly crunchy sound. If a large area of gravel looks boring, strategically position groupings of paving slabs, granite setts, railway sleepers or even glass blocks within it, to guide you down the path – perfect if you want something a little firmer underfoot.

EDGINGS

Specialist edges are important when building a loose-material path, not only as a mowing edge or as a barrier to stop materials from spilling out, but also because they define the path and emphasise its importance. Almost anything can be used as an edging as long as it's firmly secured; bed it in concrete or support it with treated wooden pegs – whichever is appropriate.

For contemporary gardens, polished metal strips give a crisp finish and, if they're slightly raised, they will reflect the paving or gravel used on the other side. For Victorian cottage-style gardens, use terracotta 'rope-top' tiles, granite setts, bricks on edge in a saw-tooth pattern, old round-ended roofing tiles, willow hoops – or whatever rustic-style edging you like.

Round sawn logs or short lengths of tree stake rammed straight into the ground suit curvy edges in naturalistic gardens, and can rise and fall in height as your whim takes you. For no effort whatsoever, simply line your paths with thick branches or railway sleepers. Dwarf hedges like box and lavender also make good edges, as do step-over apple trees.

You can edge paving slabs with a complementary material, but this is purely cosmetic and can easily over-complicate the design; if you get it wrong, it can look like a dog's dinner.

PATHS MADE OF GRAVEL OR BARK ARE EASY TO CONSTRUCT

HOW TO LAY A LOOSE PATH

• Mark out where you want your path to be, then dig down about 50mm (2in).

• Line the sides of the path with pre-treated timber planks or stones to retain the infill.

• Compact the bare soil , then lay a semi-permeable geotextile membrane on the soil to stop weeds from taking over.

• Cut the membrane to size and fashion some little metal staples out of fencing wire or coat-hangers to hold it down and stop it sliding. Overlap all the joints, otherwise you'll end up with little rows of weeds poking through.

• The depth of gravel or bark should be thin enough so it doesn't feel like you're walking on quicksand, yet deep enough so that the weed-repressing membrane doesn't show through – 50mm (2in) is usually enough, but go to nearly double that if you're laying bark for a children's play area.

• For heavy-duty paths, dig down to about 100mm (4in) and lay a 50mm (2in) sub-base of crushed hardcore or hoggin (a self-binding clay and gravel aggregate). Use a vibrating plate to compact it down thoroughly.

SOFTER SURFACES

Who wouldn't want a lawn in their garden? Not only is it a cheap, functional and child-friendly surface, a well-tended lawn is the ideal foil for some well thought-out planting. The only real drawback is that you've got to mow it.

If your garden is big enough, why not create a separate wildflower meadow that will need cutting only two or three times a year? A path cut into rough grass under a canopy of fruit trees always looks stunning, but you do need a lot of space to fully appreciate its restrained simplicity.

Astroturf and rubber are modern alternatives to grass, popular because they can be used all year round and need little maintenance. But they just ain't grass, are they?

MAKING A LAWN

Lawns are created by sowing seed in situ or by bedding down rolls of pre-cut turf. Seed is undoubtedly the cheaper option; to cover the same area using turf may cost as much as five times more. It's also easier to cover tricky shapes with seed, but it does take longer to establish. The best time to create a lawn from either turf or seed is September or March, during spells in the weather when the ground is neither frozen nor waterlogged.

Good soil preparation is essential for a lawn, so make sure that you eradicate any perennial weeds while digging over the ground. Pull them out by hand or, if that's an impossible task, use a translocated weedkiller like Round Up to knock them on the head. Dig and rake the soil till you have a fine crumbly finish or 'tilth'. For larger areas you can rent a rotovator quite cheaply. After you've cultivated the soil, it needs to be consolidated or firmed well; put on your steel-toecapped boots, place one foot next to the other, and systematically shuffle your way over the area. This will help iron out any bumps, and prevents subsidence. Rake in a general fertiliser such as Growmore, following the instructions on the packet, to help get your lawn off to the best possible start.

SOWING GRASS SEED

For ordinary lawns, buy a utility seed mix; it's hard-wearing, and suitable for all but the shadiest spots. For a naturalised meadow, buy a wildflower mix. Weigh out the specified amount, and spread it evenly over the area. Do this by hand or use a lawn spreader (available from hire shops). I always divide an area into square metres using bamboo canes; this makes it easier to spread the right amount of seed over a given area (the instructions nearly always stipulate so many grams per square metre). This way I manage to avoid bald patches. Lightly rake the seed into the soil, and water well. If any areas sprout rather thinly, just scatter a little more seed over that spot, and water in.

LAYING TURF

Although many garden centres sell turf, you will usually get better-quality turf at specialist nurseries. Always check that it's fresh (brown patches are a bad sign), that it's free from weeds and holes, that it's been cut evenly and hasn't dried out.

• Plan to lay the turf the day you buy it, but if that's not possible, unroll each piece in a shady spot and water well. Never leave rolls of turf stacked up for long periods; they won't last.

• Lay each piece in an offset pattern, like normal brickwork, and butt them up to each other, nudging the edges tightly together.

• Treading on freshly laid turf will damage it, so always work from a plank or scaffold board, which also helps firm each piece down. When you've laid the first row, just flip the board over onto it, then lay the next row, and continue until you finish.

• Use a bread knife to cut the turf to the desired shape. For curvy areas lay down a hosepipe or length of rope where you want the lawn to finish, and cut to shape.

LOOKING AFTER YOUR LAWN

Always ensure your new lawn doesn't dry out; once it's established it can look after itself. Seeded lawns should not be walked on until the seed has germinated and grown to about 5cm (2in); this usually takes six weeks. While turf may establish quite quickly, resist walking on it for a couple of weeks to give it time to root. Then mow it regularly, ideally once a week during the growing season, which is from March to October, and give it a feed every spring.

BOUNDARIES & HEIGHT

Hedges, walls and fences are more than just a boundary or a screen for privacy and security. They are important vertical design elements, bringing height to what might be a boringly flat space.

A garden that can be viewed all at once is static and holds no surprises. Long gardens especially draw the eye straight to the back fence or wall. To generate interest and an element of mystery, create diversions along the way. Position hedges, walls and fences strategically to define different 'rooms'. To create an overlying sense of unity, use materials that harmonise with your surroundings. Even the smallest garden can be made to feel larger and more interesting by breaking it up into different areas, each one having a different function or planting scheme. Create tension, tease, draw and entice the viewer in; play games with trompe l'oeil and create secluded areas.

Before putting up a tall internal division like a fence or wall, consider the shade it might cast; some shade is fine, but you don't want to eclipse the sun too much. Take the height of existing and proposed trees and shrubs into account when adding new vertical elements. A combination of too many tall features and planting will create a lack of balance. Keep proportion in mind: tall hedges in a small garden will make it feel hemmed in and smaller than it really is.

WALLS & FENCES

Walls need to be constructed properly, as safety is paramount. Unless you are building a wall no more than four or five courses high, get a bricklayer to do it for you. Fences, on the other hand, are quick and easy to erect yourself.

- Walls can be made of natural stone: flint, limestone, sandstone or mixed flint and brick.

- Disguise unsightly breeze block walls by having them rendered.

- Walls and fences are ideal for small gardens where you must think vertically with your planting. Walls provide excellent support for climbers and ramblers; run wires between vine-eyes, or secure trellis to the wall, leaving a small gap behind so that *Clematis* and other twining climbers can pull themselves up.

- Fake doors break up a long expanse of tall walling, as do trompe l'oeil windows, and make a small garden feel bigger.

- Picket fences (and hedges) filter the wind, causing less damage to plants on the other side. Walls aren't that good at sheltering you and plants from the wind; you get a buffeting effect as the wind tumbles over the top.

- Trellis, willow and picket fencing can be used to delineate areas without blocking them off completely, but they offer little privacy.

- Panel fencing creates a thin yet solid barrier; tall panels are good for privacy.

- Woven wattle, willow, and bamboo screens are excellent for rural, oriental and contemporary designs alike, but may not last as long as traditional fencing.

- Post-and-rail fences, traditionally made of oak or chestnut, are well suited to cottage and country gardens. They look stunning smothered in climbers.

HEDGES

Hedges make the perfect foil for planting, and are often used as part of the 'backbone'. Evergreens like *Prunus lusitanica* and yew give excellent year-round privacy; thorny hedges like holly give good security. Even if you want a 'quick' hedge, don't opt for the Leyland cypress – it's a monster that will require constant maintenance, annoy your neighbours and rob the surrounding soil of all nutrients. Try western red cedar instead – it smells of pineapple!

- Clipped hedges are ideal for formal gardens and give a garden a stately tone, but they will need pruning to shape three or four times a year.

- Informal hedges need little pruning – perhaps only once a year. Use flowering shrubs like *Forsythia* and *Weigela* for seasonal colour.

- Any plant can be a hedge: dwarf hedges made of lavender, box or rosemary don't give you much privacy but will define the boundaries of different 'rooms'.

- Hedges are versatile; they can be trimmed to shape, they change with the season and can support other flowering climbers rambling through them, but they take time to reach their allotted height.

- Evergreen hedges are perfect for year-round screening.

FORMAL HEDGES

Plant	Evergreen or deciduous	Planting distances	How often do I trim?
Buxus sempervirens (box)	Evergreen	30cm (12in)	2–3 times during growing season
Fagus sylvatica (beech)	Deciduous	50cm (20in)	Twice in spring/late summer
Ilex aquifolium (holly)	Evergreen	50cm (20in)	Once in late summer
Taxus baccata (yew)	Evergreen conifer	50cm (20in)	2–3 times during growing season
Thuja plicata (western red cedar)	Evergreen conifer	60cm (24in)	2–3 times in spring/late summer

INFORMAL HEDGES

Plant	Evergreen or deciduous	Planting distances	How often do I trim?
Aucuba japonica	Evergreen	60cm (24in)	Twice in spring/late summer
Escallonia macrantha	Evergreen	50cm (20in)	Once after flowering
Fargesia nitida (bamboo)	Evergreen	60cm (24in)	Remove dead wood when necessary
Fuchsia magellanica	Deciduous	50cm (20in)	Once in spring (remove dead wood)
Lavandula angustifolia (lavender)	Evergreen	30cm (12in)	Once after flowering (don't cut into old wood)

OTHER VERTICAL ELEMENTS

To define the vertical space still further, use pergolas, arches, overhead beams, arbours and tunnels. There's a huge range of ready-made structures available in numerous different styles, one of which is bound to suit your design. Most are made of metal and some use pre-treated timber, which although cheaper, doesn't last as long. I prefer metal because the supports are usually very thin; train climbers over them and it seems like they're suspended in midair! Some arches and arbours are made from woven willow stems – perfect for cottage gardens. If you're feeling particularly gung ho, you could make one out of brick or stone.

It's important to site these features carefully, so they need to be planned as an integral part of your design. They should never steal the scene, just blend in seamlessly with their surroundings. Try to avoid positioning them so they become a domineering focal point.

Pergolas, arches and open tunnels can be used to **link different parts of the garden** together, but they should always be there for a reason. It's a complete waste of money and creativity if they just show the way to a hedge or the compost heap!

Arbours and bowers, however, are static features that should be placed as focal points, attracting you to them. Positioned at the end of paths, they make perfect little spots for a bit of intimacy or seclusion. Cover them in fragrant jasmine to cast some welcome shade on hot summer days.

Overhead beams are ideal for creating outdoor rooms. Simply run joists out from the house and support them with timber posts. They'll help to **define a seating area** underneath and are perfect for some overhead privacy – just the thing if you live in a garden flat.

Sharon & Gordon's garden, Glasgow

Bristol

Cobbles and pebbles are a great way to add texture to smooth paving

Always make sure your pond or water feature is level so that water won't spill over the side

The reflective containers add interest and will help make this garden feel bigger

BRISTOL

Basement gardens aren't always gloomy: Tanith and Kay's is sunny and south-facing – a real suntrap.

Imitation natural stone paving, which was chosen to help keep the costs down, covers most of the garden, meaning that parties will never be a problem. Cut to an informal free-form shape with an angle grinder, the paving runs diagonally from the back door, creating a strong directional emphasis and leading the eye to the elegant stainless-steel water feature and weeping pear behind, which casts some welcome shade.

The three painted wooden benches provide ample seating, as well as storage; each one has a hinged lid so that garden tools can be hidden away yet still easily accessed.

The border planting is feminine with lots of silver, purples and blues among some solid evergreen structural planting for winter interest. These colours provide continuity with the interior décor, making the lounge, which overlooks the garden, appear much bigger.

Mounds of large cobbles alongside the smooth paving add contrast and texture. Box cones in containers introduce a slightly formal note and offset the frothy silver *Artemisia*, *Campanula*, *Lamium* and *Geranium* 'Johnson's Blue', which are planted throughout.

Access to the garden is restricted, so a final word of thanks to the kind neighbour who let us move our equipment through his garden.

PLANTS, PLANTS, PLANTS!

The choice of plants is bewildering, although matching up plant to place is definitely one of the more satisfying aspects of making a garden. But if you're a newcomer to this gardening malarkey, you might feel that plants are the scariest part of the process. What's out there, where can you buy them, and how might different ones work in your design? Look no further! This chapter will answer a lot of your questions.

Featured are profiles of many of my favourite plants, which are perfectly suited to city gardens – I've used many of them in *The City Gardener* TV series on Channel 4. You'll find loads of info about how to grow them successfully and ideas about where to plant them, plus the checks you should make to ensure you're buying a plant that's raring to go! These plants work well in all kinds of situations and fulfil many different functions. Browse through the various categories and see if any of them take your fancy.

Just a quick note, so you don't get confused: the terms 'cultivar' and 'variety' essentially mean the same thing. A cultivar is a cultivated variety.

BUYING PLANTS

Most of us get our plants from garden centres, nurseries and supermarkets, but the cheapest way is to swap plants with your neighbours – and you know that plants from their gardens will probably grow just as well in yours. Most gardeners are a good-hearted bunch, only too happy to give you cuttings from prize shrubs, or clumps they've cut from their herbaceous perennials. You will have to spend some money eventually, though – no one's going to part with a prized Japanese maple!

Depending upon the time of year, you can buy plants in containers, bare-rooted, root-balled or pre-packed in cellophane or plastic.

CONTAINER-GROWN PLANTS

The advantage of plants grown in containers is that they can be bought and planted at any time of year, as long as the ground isn't frozen or waterlogged. Most are priced according to the size of the container, which is measured in litres. Herbaceous perennials are commonly grown in two-litre pots, whereas shrubs, climbers, grasses and bamboos are generally available in three- or five-litre pots, and trees in 10-, 12- or 15-litre containers – all of which are easy to handle. (If you want to know the size of the pot, just look on the bottom where the size will be inscribed in the plastic.) The range of ornamental plants grown in plastic pots is vast, but the downside is they can be quite pricey because growers have to factor-in the costs of the container itself, the compost, controlled-release fertiliser, as well as the time spent putting the plant in the container, .

Although buying your container-grown plants from reputable sources will usually be fine, it's still worth knowing what makes a quality plant, and how to spot one. You don't want to waste your money on a plant that's going to die on you!

Always check that the plant is firm in its pot. Hold the base of the main stem and give it a *gentle* tug. If the plant comes out easily, be wary: either the plant hasn't established well in its container or it could have been recently potted on, meaning that you'll have to wait a while before you can successfully plant it out. Another reason might be a lack of basic watering. Then ease the plant out of its container and give the roots the once-over. If you see thick matted roots winding around the root-ball, with hardly any compost visible, then the plant is pot-bound, which means it should have been potted on into a larger container. This is not a good specimen to buy. The roots will eventually strangle the plant, or they might not reach out into the good soil in your garden.

If you see lots of young white feeder roots just starting to show through the soil, that's a good sign. It indicates the plant is a young specimen, that it hasn't used up all the nutrients in the pot and is ready to rocket away when you plant it.

As with all container plants, take care if you spot obvious signs of neglect such as bone-dry compost, masses of weeds or little white larvae, which could be the dreaded vine weevil.

Above the ground you want a bushy, compact plant with lots of new shoots that are evenly spread out. Avoid plants whose leaves look pale, shrivelled, or distorted – all of which are signs of malnourishment. Check for uncharacteristic spots, odd unhealthy-looking marks on the stems, mould, leaves smothered in whitefly (easy to spot because they are tiny white flies), bugs and tiny red-brown spider mites and their thin matted webs covering the leaves or stems. If you desperately want a plant because it's the only one left, ask yourself why it's the nursery wallflower – don't be tempted!

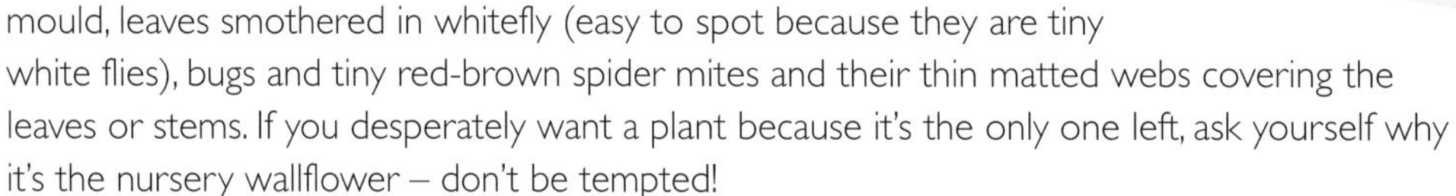

BARE-ROOTED PLANTS

Lots of people are scared to buy bare-rooted plants, thinking they are bound to die on them. But if you can get hold of them at the right time, they're a worthy alternative to container-grown plants. You'll find them sold only between October and March after the grower has carefully lifted them from the ground. The lifting and planting of bare-root stock must be done in winter when the plant is dormant and soil conditions permit. Invariably the choice is limited to broad-leaved trees and shrubs, fruit, roses and occasionally herbaceous perennials.

I always prefer to go to specialist nurseries direct for bare-rooted plants, especially when searching for rare apples, cherries, plums and obscure roses, which have been grown in this way for aeons. Kindly sorts will allow you to tramp their fields and mark the plants you want yourself – just make sure you wear your wellies!

You might ask why you should bother to buy bare-rooted plants when they are only available for just a few months of the year. To start with, they're a lot cheaper. Many plants growing in containers were once grown in the field and have simply been potted up, or 'containerised'. This puts up the price. By going straight to the source, the cost can be reduced by half (a bit like cutting out the middleman). For this reason most deciduous hedging is sold bare-root; making a hedge uses a lot of plants, and if they're all container-grown, the cost will be crippling. Plants grown in the field will also establish more readily because the roots have been allowed to spread as they're supposed to. They'll put on far more growth in their first year than you might ever expect.

If you buy bare-rooted plants, always check that the roots aren't damaged too much. The lifting process can be brutal: a couple of snapped roots is nothing to worry about, but if half the roots have been ripped off, then simply choose another plant. Look for plants with a well-developed root system that spreads out in a radial pattern, with lots and lots of fine brown feeder roots. Most important, the roots of recently lifted plants should be covered at all times – they MUST NOT be allowed to dry out. Although the plant is not actively growing, the roots will dry out fast if they're exposed to the air; if they do, the plant will die. Use soil, damp straw, old carpet, anything – just keep those roots covered. When you're actually in the process of planting out bare-rooted plants, dunk them in a large container of water until it's time to put them in the ground to reinvigorate the roots and help the tree to establish well.

If you're buying a bare-rooted tree, make sure the head has been pruned to a good shape, that it's not lopsided, that any grafts are neat, there's no obvious damage to the trunk, and that there are no dead or damaged shoots. Avoid those with lots of branches that cross each other as they'll rub together and create wounds through which disease can enter.

ROOT-BALLED PLANTS

Evergreens and conifers never go dormant in the same way as deciduous plants, so field-grown stock can't be lifted bare-root but have to be lifted with a root-ball. The plant is removed from the ground with the soil intact around the roots, and the root-ball is then wrapped tightly with hessian. Larger specimens are usually wrapped in chain-link fencing as well, to stop the root-ball from disintegrating.

The size of the root-ball depends upon the type of soil in which the plant was grown, and the species and the size of the plant. In any case, the grower will try to preserve as much of the root system as possible. As a result root-balled plants establish well – sometimes it seems as if the plant doesn't even realise that it's been moved!

Root-balled plants are generally available in early spring. But unlike plants lifted bare-root, which should be planted as soon as possible, you have a couple of weeks' grace, provided that you keep the root-ball shaded and moist. Just remember to *always* remove the hessian and chainlink once the plant is in the planting hole.

When buying, check the condition of the root-ball. Is it dried out? Has it broken apart? Are there lots of large roots poking through the hessian? If there are, it's likely the root-ball is too small for the plant. I always look for the largest root-ball I can find; this should give you a plant with as many roots as possible. When you carry your plant to the car, make sure you carry it by the root ball and not by the main stem or the root-ball will fall apart under its own weight. Grab the root-ball itself and cradle it against your stomach; just make sure you're not wearing your best clothes!

PRE-PACKED PLANTS

Common in supermarkets and hardware stores, pre-packed plants usually come in sealed plastic bags with moist peat strapped around the roots. Buying plants this way is the least favourable option and a bit of a minefield, unless you really know how to tell a bargain from a dud. Cheap shrubs and climbers are sold in this way but, as always, you get what you pay for. Pre-packaged plants are classic 'impulse' buys, and even the most experienced gardeners often struggle to get them established.

If you must buy them, check that the plants inside haven't started growing yet. You often see roses with long white etiolated shoots winding around the inside of the packet searching for natural light – it's heartbreaking. Similarly, avoid those with lots of little white roots – this is a sign that the plant's been in its plastic prison too long. Aim to buy and put your plants in the ground on the same day, except in the middle of winter – when plants have been in a hot, dry supermarket for ages, they will need acclimatising slowly to the outdoors.

SIZE CAN MATTER

Gardening snobs insist that all your plants should be raised and nurtured from either seed or cuttings, and to do otherwise is sacrilege. It's true that half the fun of gardening is producing and growing your own plants but, if you've no evergreens, no backbone planting, nothing to start with, why wait for five years or more for your garden to mature? Impatient gardeners (like me) love big plants because they add a sense of scale to a new design, plus they help to create that 'been-there-for-years' look. They're also perfect if privacy or security is a problem and you need an instant solution.

Many nurseries specialise in large plants and they are worth a visit. Choose a nursery recommended in the better gardening magazines or by professional gardeners – growing and handling plants as tall as double-decker buses involves a fair degree of skill. After you've had a good look around, sit down with a stiff drink. The biggest of the biggies are going to make a huge hole in your wallet. Giants aside, you'll still be able to pick up something in a 30–40 litre pot about 4m (13ft) tall for a decent price. Just come armed with your site survey so you can ask the grower for expert advice if you need to.

Plan for a few friends to give you a hand planting a big specimen. The pot might prove very tough to remove. More often than not, you sacrifice the pot. Lay the plant on its side and then, using a knife, slice up the side of the pot, being careful obviously not to cut through too many roots!

Choosing and buying big plants isn't the hard bit, though – it's getting them home and into the garden. Most nurseries will offer a delivery service, and this way your plants will get home in one piece, instead of sticking out through the sunroof, leaves trailing behind you like a comet. Through bitter experience I now always take along a tape measure – just to make sure I can get the plant through any side access or front door. Don't leave it to chance, there's nothing more embarrassing!

TREES

Don't underestimate the importance of trees, especially in the urban garden where they provide shade, privacy, tranquillity, as well as help fight pollution. Yes, many may be huge and downright scary, but there are loads that aren't and that would suit even the smallest backyard. With a tree, your garden gains an air of substance and maturity – ideal if your budget is tight.

Design-wise, trees can act as natural focal points. However, they also work well planted among shrubs, conifers and herbaceous plants, where they create a sense of proportion and scale, subsequently enhancing any design. If you're trying to 'break up' an otherwise open garden, use trees to help create secret hideaways and somewhere to chill out in private.

In an overcrowded urban environment trees are excellent at screening. Planted close together, they work well as a barrier or hedge. A tree or large shrub will always look better than a high fence or wall for screening that builders' yard at the bottom of the garden. Evergreens, such as *Magnolia grandiflora*, with its whopping great creamy white fragrant flowers, are perfect for year-round screening, and much more interesting than a brown fence! If shade is your craving, then trees with small leaves like the purple birch (*Betula pendula* 'Purpurea') or *Laburnum* x *watereri* 'Vossii' are ideal.

THE LOW DOWN...

Most trees will need a hefty stake hammered into the ground (though not through their roots!) and special tree-ties to anchor them securely when you plant them. The planting hole should be at least double the size of the root-ball. If you're planting bare-root, it's especially important that the hole is wide enough for the root system to fit in easily. Always plant to the same depth as the tree was planted before (look at the bottom of the trunk for telltale signs). Fill the hole with compost-enriched soil to give the new roots a great head start.

Newly planted trees need looking after. In the first two years you must water them if the soil is dry, and with hotter drier summers forecast, this is essential. Soak the soil around the roots so they spread out, and give them a couple of watering-canfuls each time you water – this may be every few days in extremely hot weather. After the first two years most trees can take care of themselves.

• Remember to take into account the eventual size of the tree. It may look small when you plant it, but how big will it be in ten years' time?

• Never plant Leyland cypress (x *Cupressocyparis leylandii*) unless you're absolutely desperate – it will quickly turn into a monster!

• Think about the features that you'd like your tree to have. Do you want flowers, autumn colour, bark or scent – or a tree that has a bit of everything?

• Trees with a good winter silhouette and bark, such as *Prunus serrula*, *Acer davidii* and *Betula utilis* var. *jacquemontii*, look stunning during the miserable months of the year.

• Choose carefully and you can grow a tree in a large container. The Japanese maples are ideal for this, as are magnolias and even birches. Make sure that you use a heavy container, such as one made of concrete, for permanent plantings because lighter ones can easily blow over.

• Don't plant trees with invasive roots (willows, limes and eucalyptus) near buildings. Your nursery will always advise you about this.

• For year-round privacy or interest, don't forget evergreens; they really come into their own in winter.

Acer davidii

Père David's maple, named after the French missionary who discovered it in its native China, is famed for its streaked green and white bark, which really attracts the eye in winter. Growing to 15m (50ft), it's also renowned for its spectacular autumn colour, especially on acid soils, when the leaves turn yellow and orange before falling. The stem colour is best on younger wood, making it a good container plant. Requiring rich neutral to acid, well-drained soil, 'Serpentine' (pictured) thrives in part-shade. For bright orange autumn colour, 'Ernest Wilson' is a must. Other acers with fantastic winter bark include *A. rufinerve*, whose leaves turn bright red in autumn, and *A. griseum*, the paper-bark maple, with peeling orange-brown bark.

Albizia julibrissin 'Rosea'

Also called the Persian acacia, this is a slightly tender, delicate-looking tree. It really only succeeds in the south of the country, and even then it needs full sun and the hottest, most protected wall you have. This isn't so much to guard it against frost, because it can survive a few degrees of it, but in order to ripen the wood. Enclosed sunny city courtyards fit the bill perfectly! Even when young, its long acacia-like, finely divided leaves of light/mid-green are eye-catching, revealing a golden tinge when sunlight filters through them. In late summer it bears dense clusters of bright fluffy pink bottlebrush flowers – quite extraordinary! Eventually, the tree will reach an attractive dome 9m (30ft) in height and spread, but don't let that worry you – it's no triffid.

Amelanchier lamarckii

Snowy mespillus, a native of eastern North America, bears a profusion of massed clusters of delicate white spring blossom just as its leaves begin to emerge a pale pink-bronze. This spectacular flush of star-shaped flowers tends to be short-lived, though reliable, and is followed in late summer by an almost equally spectacular fiery red and orange autumn leaf show. Midsummer provides a flush of small red berries, which later turn black; these are edible but hardly table-worthy. Commonly growing to a height and spread of 4.5m (15ft), it thrives in ordinary, preferably lime-free, well-drained – but not dry – soil in an open sunny or slightly shady position. To get the best from its blazing autumn glory, place it in full sun. It complements copper-leaved shrubs, magnolias and evergreens.

Betula utilis var. *jacquemontii*

Use the West Himalayan birch, with its dazzling white bark, to brighten up the dull winter months. Typical of the birch family, it has an elegant open habit, and its small leaves cast little shade in summer. Eventually reaching 15m (50ft) high, it is a slow-grower, tolerant of most soils, including chalk, although it does best on moderately acid moist soils. It likes an open or partially shaded position, and does well in urban areas. Alternative birches include *B. papyrifera*, the paper birch, whose waterproof white bark was used by Native Americans for their canoes, and *B. pendula*, the silver birch, with its graceful pendulous shape so beloved of country gardens. Grown close together, these birches create a fabulous miniature woodland look.

Cercidiphyllum japonicum

The multi-stemmed katsura will grow to about 15m (50ft) tall with a spread of 10m (33ft), so will need some space. The small heart-shaped leaves are a delightful bronzy colour as they unfurl in spring, ultimately turning pale green in summer. In autumn the foliage colours beautifully into brilliant shades of gold, orange and red. When the leaves fall they give off the delicious smell of burnt sugar, which is, quite literally, like walking into a sweet factory… hence its other common name, the candyfloss tree. *Cercidiphyllum japonicum* does need some protection as cold winds and early spring frosts will cause serious damage to the young delicate shoots. For the best leaf colour it needs a moist fertile slightly acid soil, but it will tolerate alkaline or dry soils, especially if they're mulched regularly.

Cornus controversa 'Variegata'

The table dogwood isn't at all controversial, as its name suggests, but it does show off its branches in flat tiers like layered tabletops. With its twisted – the 'controversa' bit – green and white variegated foliage, and flat panicles of creamy white flowers, you have a wedding cake up to 8m (26ft) tall. The flowers appear in spring; in winter the stems turn a deep plum-purple. Requiring an open or lightly shaded position, it's tolerant of most soils. Like *Viburnum plicatum* 'Mariesii', whose tiered symmetry is even more striking, it associates well with columnar and rounded shapes; try it next to bronze *Phormium tenax*, dark green topiary balls of box or the arching stems of the bamboo *Sinarundinaria murieliae*. But to appreciate its magnificent shape fully, grow it on its own.

Hamamelis mollis

Chinese witch hazel is a winter must-have. In the dullest months it is festooned with frost-resistant bright yellow spidery flowers, which give off a heady spicy fragrance, rather like marmalade! All its cultivars have an open vase shape and do best in light shade; 'Pallida' is slightly more upright, with dense clusters of large sulphur-yellow flowers. Slow-growing, witch hazels will reach a height and spread of 4m (12ft). They all prefer rich deep, well-drained acid soils, but will tolerate chalk with a good covering of humus. The autumn foliage colours nicely but can be reluctant to drop. They also suit containers, provided they are well watered. Underplant with grape hyacinths, dwarf daffodils and other small spring bulbs. This is definitely a tree to give the garden, and the gardener, a touch of real class.

***Laburnum x watereri* 'Vossii'**

With such beautiful flowers, there has to be a downside to laburnums – they have poisonous seeds. 'Vossii', though, sets practically no seed, so it's relatively safe if there are young children around, and you still have the long dense pendulous racemes of rich yellow pea flowers in late spring. It grows to 6 x 4.5m (20 x 15ft) and is a real show stopper when in full flower (visit the fantastic laburnum tunnel at Bodnant Garden Nursery in Colwyn Bay in May). It's best as a focal point, perfect in the centre of a lawn, where the flowers are seen to full effect. When not in flower, the small delicate three-lobed leaves are attractive in their own right. It likes a well-drained soil in a sunny open position. The wood is highly prized by wood-turners for furniture-making, but who would want to cut it down?

***Morus alba* 'Pendula'**

Mulberries were first introduced into Britain by James I in the early 17th century, in the hope of establishing a silk industry – the leaves of the white mulberry (*Morus alba*) are the silkworm's staple diet. But the king got it wrong and introduced the black mulberry (*M. nigra*) by mistake; some of these original introductions still survive. 'Pendula', the weeping white mulberry, is ideal for small spaces, growing to no more than 3 x 5m (10 x 15ft). It's self-fertile, producing edible fleshy pink/red/purple oval fruits in summer, which, though good raw, are probably best for jam. The heart-shaped leaves are deep glossy green, taking on yellow autumn tints. Your weeping mulberry might just support silkworms if you want your own cottage industry!

Prunus 'Kanzan'

The name 'Kanzan' relates to the Chinese character that represents a sacred mountain. This fine flowering cherry is almost neglected by gardeners because it's used so much in municipal planting. It's a tree that's not noted for its subtlety: the extravagance of flowering is jaw-dropping, and in early spring it's literally smothered in pale pink blossom. With its upright shape and bare lower trunk, 'Kanzan' looks especially good with an underpinning of early spring bulbs. The long-toothed leaves open a dark reddish colour, turn dull green for summer and then take on golden and red tints in autumn. It likes most soils in a sunny open aspect, and is tolerant of pollution, which is why you see it so often planted in town and city streets.

Prunus serrula

This oriental cherry, a native of western China, is grown mainly for its polished mahogany-red peeling bark. Tree-huggers beware: it's impossible to pass it by without running your hand over the shiny smooth bark. Reaching a height and spread of 10m (30ft), this majestic round-headed tree looks best on its own in the centre of a lawn or bordering a path, where you can admire its bark close-up. As a bonus, its toothed tapering oval dark green leaves turn yellow in autumn. It prefers full sun and an open aspect, and is tolerant of all soils, as long as they're not waterlogged. For elegant flowering cherries, try *P. subhirtella* 'Autumnalis', a small delicate beauty that flowers in milder spells from autumn to spring, or *P. mume*, the Japanese apricot, which has scented pink flowers in late winter.

Sorbus cashmiriana

The Kashmir rowan grows to 8m (26ft) and, typical of the rowan family, is smothered in dense clusters of berries from late summer to winter. In this case the berries are gleaming white, showing strongly against the golden yellow autumn foliage. Well-behaved trees, rowans don't cast deep shade, have pretty divided leaflets, bear a flush of pale pink flowers in late spring and look best in the middle of a lawn as solitary specimens. They do best in open sunny positions, in moist humus-rich soil. *Sorbus hupehensis* is similar, with white flowers in early summer, good autumn colour, and whitish-pink berries in autumn. Both trees hold onto their berries until late into winter, well after leaf fall, unlike the red-berried cultivars whose fruits are quickly eaten by birds.

EVERGREENS • ARCHITECTURAL SHRUBS

Evergreens are backbone plants that give the garden its form and structure, so think about this group early on in the design process. They are great for giving you year-round privacy, and you should make them your first choice for screening out an eyesore. Choice evergreens like *Griselinia littoralis*, *Pittosporum tenuifolium* and spotted laurel (*Aucuba japonica*) also make great hedges, protecting windswept gardens from adverse weather. Use striking architectural evergreen shrubs as focal points in winter and when you want to make a statement in the garden.

DEPENDABLE BUDDIES

Evergreens are solid and reliable, and will always give you some colour. You may not pay much attention to them in summer, but in winter you will! Always include evergreens in a basic planting plan, and remember that not all these plants are green: some have gold or variegated leaves, like *Elaeagnus pungens* 'Maculata' or *Choisya ternata* 'Sundance', to really brighten up the winter garden. *Sarcococca* and *Mahonia* have scent in winter, too.

SHOW-OFFS!

Evergreen architectural plants give the garden a solid substantial feel, anchor it and help shape its character. Among them you can count *Euphorbia*, *Phormium*, *Fatsia* and pencil junipers, which are particularly striking in appearance. There's always an element of ego among these architectural plants, whether it's their eye-catching form, bigger-than-average leaves or strange flowers. Planted en masse in a small space like a city courtyard, they'll create a jungly atmosphere, but in certain schemes beware of using too many as their impact may be lost. As well as these aggressive 'notice-me' characters, there are some more demure individuals, like *Acacia dealbata* (mimosa).

• Evergreens need little maintenance – no pruning, just a bit of Growmore or organic fertiliser scattered around them in spring.

• Box (*Buxus*) or clipped shrubby honeysuckle (*Lonicera nitida*) in containers looks the biz! For detailed shapes, simply use chicken wire to create a 3-D outline and trim accordingly.

Variegated Phormium & Pittosporum tobira 'Nanum'

• A lot of evergreens have shiny leaves that reflect light. Try to include these rather than the matt-leaved varieties, which can look depressingly dull in winter.

• Use architectural plants as exclamation marks in the garden – in places where you want to be surprised or that you want to draw attention to.

• If you have a group of modest plants, none of which stands out in any way, but overall they create a pleasant effect, just try adding a plant with drama. This will set the whole group talking. Architectural plants contrast and catalyse so that duller plants around them borrow from their impact.

• Evergreens are great for repetition. For formal, think a row of box balls or upright junipers (*Juniperus scopulorum* 'Skyrocket') lining the path leading up to your house or defining a patio. For informal, think clipped meandering mounds of evergreen azaleas, as in Japanese gardens.

• When planting evergreens, water them well and continue to do so right through their first summer. It's hard to tell if an evergreen is ailing until it goes brown and looks really awful – by which time it's often too late.

Camellia japonica

Camellias have one specific requirement: neutral to acid soil. If you have chalk, don't despair; smaller cultivars do well in half-barrels or heavy pots of ericaceous compost. Related to the tea plant, which gives us the cuppa, camellias are glossy-leaved evergreens with large cup- or bowl-shaped flowers in singles and doubles, in colours from white, through all the pinks, to red. Correct siting is important. They like a sheltered position and protection from winter winds, so growing them against walls is ideal (but not east-facing ones, where the early morning sun might damage their frosted flowers). They tolerate pollution and shade, so are ideal for city gardens. 'Adolphe Audusson' (pictured) forms a 3.7m (12ft) high pyramid, sporting clear red semi-double flowers from February to May.

Chamaerops humilis

The European fan palm is a slow-growing evergreen, eventually reaching a height of 1.5m (5ft), with fan-shaped leaves measuring 1m (3ft) across. It is slightly tender, surviving temperatures to around –5°C (23°F), but it can also be kept in a conservatory or greenhouse over winter and put out as the weather warms up – this shouldn't be necessary in small protected urban settings. Grown in a decorative pot, it makes a fine accent on the patio or decking, and needs little maintenance. It does need a fertile well-drained soil and full sun to do well. Don't overwater or it will soon rot. Red spider mite can be a problem so, before you buy, give the plant a good once-over at the garden centre to avoid importing this pest into your garden.

Choisya ternata 'Sundance'

Everyone was content with plain old green-leaved *Choisya ternata* until this golden Mexican orange blossom came along – nurseries couldn't get enough of it! Like most yellow-leaved varieties, 'Sundance' is not as vigorous as its parent; eventually it will reach 2.5m (8ft) or so, forming a neat dense mound. The leaves, a shiny mid-yellow, draw the eye, even when the plant is small, and the star-shaped blossom in April/May is a bonus: fine creamy white heads, sweetly scented. The leaves, if you crush them, are also scented. 'Sundance' needs a more sheltered spot than its parent, and will get windburn (brown edges and browning of the leaves) in an exposed position. A mixed border or shrub border in sun suits it well, though it will also thrive in light shade if the site is sheltered.

Euphorbia characias subsp. _wulfenii_
The architect's architectural plant and almost a cliché in gravel gardens, this heat-loving evergreen has a primitive aggressiveness about its appearance when in flower. It has blue-green leaves on shoots 1.2–1.8m (4–6ft) high and forms a neat rounded shape. In spring the flowers appear as a continuation of the stems, like huge lime-green bottlebrushes punching the air. Up close the tiny individual flowers have a brown eye. These stay on the plant until the end of July, when they fade and need to be cut off. All the *Euphorbia* have architectural merit, from the small round *E. polychroma*, with its bright yellow bracts, to the scented and slightly tender *E. mellifera*. In general, euphorbias like full sun and well-drained soils. Just be careful of their milky sap, which is a skin irritant.

Fargesia nitida (syn. _Sinarundinaria nitida_)
Well behaved for a bamboo, and remaining in a clump, the fountain bamboo makes an ideal specimen plant, a hedge with a difference or a whispering screen, but it also looks good in a pot. Fully hardy, *F. nitida* grows some 4m (12ft) tall in an upright vase shape. It has purple-green stems; these are covered with a bluish-white powder when young. The leaves are mid/dark green. Although it appreciates having its feet moist, it will grow in drier soil. If you grow it in a container, it will need a lot of water; a large saucer underneath the pot is vital in summer. When the plant is too dry, the leaves will curl up to conserve moisture. 'Wakehurst' has larger leaves than the species. Half-shade suits this bamboo well, though it also likes a sunny spot.

Fatsia japonica
This large evergreen shrub with big palmate leaves looks like an exotic house plant. In fact, it's related to ivy and comes from Japan. A character heavyweight, this is not one to sulk in a corner. Sheltered courtyards are ideal, as are dense jungly areas around formal ponds, but don't plant it in a border or among herbs – it'll look like a beached whale! The thick stems grow to 3m (10ft) high, and carry glossy hand-shaped leaves so wide they could slap you! It does best against a wall in light shade in any well-drained soil. In autumn, each stem tip bears bosses of creamy ivy-like flowers. It will tolerate a few degrees of frost when mature, though it might droop alarmingly – don't worry, it'll soon come round. Choose 'Variegata' if space is really tight. Small plants need protection in winter.

PLANT PROFILES EVERGREENS · ARCHITECTURAL SHRUBS

***Juniperus* x *media* 'Pfitzeriana Aurea'**

Golden junipers can be chameleonic, changing colour with the seasons. This Chinese juniper has golden yellow foliage in summer, which changes to green-gold in winter. Vigorous and wide-spreading, it reaches a height and spread of 2m (7ft), and likes a well-drained spot that is slightly acid. For the most striking golden colour, it needs full sun but will grow happily in semi-shade as long as the soil is fertile. (Blue and silver-green junipers look better in semi-shade.) Its branches arch up and branch out gracefully. 'Mint Julep' is a deep rich mid-green and a fast-growing flat-spreading bush. Junipers can survive hot dry places well. They have a gin-like aroma when the leaves are crushed! Plant as a lone specimen or with other contrasting columnar shapes.

Phormium tenax

The bold New Zealand flax has many tough sword-shaped leaves shooting out of a clump, giving it an arresting and slightly ferocious apppearance. Modern gravel gardens and minimalist designs embrace it well because of its strong linear form. Think of it as a catalyst to other forms, as well as being a dominant individual in its own right. Whatever, it repays considered positioning. You will love it if your garden theme is contemporary, when it looks good with euphorbias, especially *E.* 'Fireglow', which will create a gentler sea of green and red around the base. Some *Phormium* are striped with orange and pink, like 'Dazzler'. They grow slowly, to 2m (6ft), and like a hot spot with well-drained soil. Severe frost kills these plants, but they usually shoot again from the base.

Phyllostachys aurea

Known also as the fishtail, or golden, bamboo, this is a frost-hardy clump-forming evergreen. The young stems, which look like green spears as they emerge from the ground, can grow to 3–4.5m (10–15ft) in the garden. They like rich deep moist porous loam, and prefer sheltered sunny or shady positions. The stems are bright golden yellow-green, brighter in full sun, and have curious distorted lower nodes. All bamboos have an effortless oriental elegance, adding a Zen calm to the garden. There are some rogues that spread and colonise indiscriminately, but many don't. They all suit containers well, even when young. Plants are expensive but you can split them up in spring when they get too big for the pot, although you may need a saw to prize the roots apart!

Pittosporum

Pittosporum are evergreen shrubs grown for their foliage and scented flowers. Many border on hardiness and will be damaged by frost, so in colder areas grow them against a south- or west-facing wall. *Pittosporum tobira* (pictured) is a seductively scented summer-flowering species, which pumps out a heavy orange-blossom fragrance from its white flowers, and is very drought-resistant. It needs mild winters, however, to do well. 'Nanum' is a smaller, more compact cultivar. *Pittosporum tenuifolium* is much tougher, with dark purple flowers and a strong honey fragrance in spring. There are also variegated silver, golden and purple forms. 'Garnettii' has a dense columnar habit, reaching 6m (20ft), with rounded grey-green leaves edged white, sometimes tinged pink. It makes an unusually attractive hedge.

Prunus laurocerasus 'Otto Luyken'

Laurels live Cinderella lives much of the time as evergreen hedging, and very good they are, too – but used in this way they are seldom noticed. This particular cherry laurel will make a magnificent specimen plant if allowed to step out of the wings. It has dark green shiny leaves, which remind you of the culinary bay tree (*Laurus nobilis*), but don't put them in your cooking pot! The leaves are also highly reflective, meaning that they lighten rather than depress. If you have plenty of space, position 'Otto Luyken' at the edge of a lawn. In April the long oval leaves are decorated with white flower spikes, 8–13cm (3–5in) long, which look like small horse-chestnut flowers. Unlike its bigger cousins, 'Otto Luyken' is a tidy plant, perfect for small gardens, with a height and spread of 1.2–1.5m (4–5 ft).

Sarcococca

For most of the year you will, frankly, not notice this genus of small-leaved evergreen shrubs! Called Christmas box, they seldom flower in the festive season, but their small leaves do resemble box (*Buxus*). So, why include this moper-no-hoper here? Well, everything to its own time, and, for *Sarcococca*, this is winter/early spring, when they give the most welcome of surprises: a sweet and penetrating scent. Plant them next to a path or near the front door to halt your chilly guests in their tracks. *Sarcococca confusa* is perhaps the most fragrant, but grows to 2m (6ft) tall. Following the flowers are clusters of glossy black fruit. *Sarcococca ruscifolia* (pictured) has red fruit and grows to half that size. Grow dwarf *S. humilis* as groundcover *Sarcococca* do best in moisture-retentive soil, in shade.

DECIDUOUS SHRUBS • ROSES

Using a variety of deciduous shrubs and roses with different seasons of flowering will help ensure year-round interest in a border. But get the balance right between evergreens and deciduous shrubs/roses: too many deciduous plants will make the garden look bare for half the year. If you love roses above all others, grow them together in one area, for a bold dramatic statement.

DECIDUOUS SHRUBS

Deciduous shrubs typically provide most of the bulk in a mixed border or infill. They can be used as solitary specimens, hedging, for covering walls and other structures, or as groundcover and subjects for whimsical topiary. Many are suitable for containers. Deciduous shrubs are often used as seasonal focal points, particularly if they have dramatic foliage or unusual flowers. The variety is enormous, and many have unusual leaf shapes or foliage that ranges from silver to deep purple to bright yellow. Some, like buddleia, need drastic pruning, while others, such as magnolia, require just a general tidy up to retain their shape. A particularly pleasing shrub that is destined eventually for the garden can first be enjoyed as a temporary container plant – in some cases for years.

ROSES

Roses are seasonal plants, and there are many types, from single-stemmed prim hybrid-teas, through multiflowered floribundas and blowsy old roses, to climbers and ramblers. It's a good idea to study a book specifically dedicated to roses. All have different pruning needs, with shrub roses requiring minimal pruning, and hybrid teas drastic pruning, every spring. In general, old-fashioned shrub roses and floribundas look good in mixed borders, while hybrid teas are better in a bed all to themselves. Some roses have one flush of flowers, others repeat-flower throughout summer and into autumn. With the exception of dwarf miniatures, most roses don't do well in containers, as they have long tap roots and are greedy feeders.

Rosa rugosa

• All roses perk up with fertiliser, especially those that are hard-pruned. Use Growmore, seaweed or even tomato fertiliser.

• Cutting off the faded roses encourages new flowers to form; don't do this if you want rose hips.

• If rose suckers emerge from the base of the plant and look different from the rest of the plant, pull them off.

• Several roses have been specially bred for containers, including window boxes, and are called patio roses. Try the dwarf 'Dresden Doll', 'Peachy White' and 'Regensberg'.

• Small repeat-flowering roses especially suit small city gardens; try a group called the Portland roses, especially 'Jacques Cartier', 'Rose de Rescht' and 'Comte de Chambord'.

• I like species and wild roses, most of which are disease-resistant and tough. Try *R.* 'Dupontii' or *R. eglanteria*, which has leaves that smell of green apples. For tiny gardens, try the miniature *R. serafinii*, with its resinous foliage, or *R. pulverulenta*, with small pink flowers and large red hips.

• Make your roses work hard for their space in a small garden: choose those with scent and a long flowering season.

• Roses can be used as groundcover. Try 'Cardinal Hume', 'Max Graf' and 'Scintillation', all of which are scented.

Abeliophyllum distichum

Often called the white forsythia, this rounded deciduous shrub is actually not forsythia, but a near relation. With a stiff multi-stemmed shape, it grows rapidly to produce arching branches some 1.5m (5ft) long. Flowering is early and susceptible to damage from hard frosts; the white, slightly fragrant, flowers emerge from purple buds to cover the naked stems in March before the leaves unfold. The flowers are crowded and so profuse, they immediately make you think 'spring blossom'. Prune directly after flowering because the new growth that results will carry next year's blooms. After flowering the shrub looks rather dull, so it's best grown among other evergreens. *Abeliophyllum* are easy to grow and, given a sheltered position in sun/partial shade, will reach 2m (7ft).

Buddleia davidii

The butterfly bush is a fast-growing deciduous shrub, easily growing 2m (6ft) a year, that is particularly useful in the newly established garden for giving early maturity. They are tough plants, preferring full sun, and will grow in any free-draining garden soil, including chalk (and railways sidings). For the best flush of summer flowers, cut back hard in early spring (chop the stems right down until you feel guilty!) because it flowers on growth made in the new season. (Other species, like *B. alternifolia* and *B. globosa*, flower on the previous season's growth, so don't need pruning as hard.) Colours can be lilac, purple, red and white. 'Royal Red' (pictured) has long bright red flower panicles and, like most *Buddleia*, is scented. All *Buddleia* attract butterflies, hence the common name.

Cornus alba

My favourite dogwood 'Sibirica' (pictured) is grown for the striking colour of its winter stems, which need cutting back to ground level in early spring to encourage bright red new growth the following year. Coppicing in this way means they shouldn't grow taller than 2m (6ft). The deciduous dogwood needs moist soil, an open or shady position and full sun for the best stem colour; choose *C. stolonifera* 'Flaviramea' for yellow stems. Inconspicuous yellow/white flowers are borne in May/June, followed by white berries, then brilliant red or orange autumn leaves. *Cornus alba* 'Variegata' has pale green leaves with a white edge and brilliant red stems on the new growth; 'Spaethii', yellow-margined leaves and bluish-white berries. Dogwoods are tough, withstanding air pollution and wind exposure.

Cotinus coggygria

The smoke tree always makes me think of magicians conjuring fantastical oddities from a hat, and this is definitely a shrub with a mystical flavour! 'Royal Purple' (pictured) has oval dark plum-purple leaves, which turn a dramatic red colour in autumn, but it's the extraordinary reddish-purple flowers that give the shrub its smoky handle. These appear to pour from the leaves in summer in a great mass of hairy spikes, so airy and fluffy that they seem to puff away from the tree in a smoke-like haze. 'Flame' has dark green foliage, turning red in autumn, while the flower plumes are tinged with pink. *Cotinus* like ordinary well-drained, even dry, soil in full sun. Don't feed them too much; it diminishes the autumn colours. Some reach a height and spread of 5m (16ft), to resemble a small branching tree.

Euonymus alatus

Also known as the winged spindle tree, this is a curiosity of a shrub that should be grown more often. A deciduous twiggy plant native to Japan, Korea and northeast China, it will grow to 2–3m (6–8ft). It earns its place in the garden because of its curious winged corky outgrowths along the stems and its amazing luminous hot pinky-red autumn colour. This is just the thing to brighten up the garden when everything else is beginning to look decidedly boring! The red fruits are a curiosity, too, opening up to reveal bright orange seeds. What a wacky colour combination on one plant! The 6mm- (¼in-) wide flowers appear in May and June, and are pale green with four petals – not the plant's strong point! Easy to grow in sun or partial shade, *E. alatus* really looks after itself.

Hydrangea arborescens 'Grandiflora'

Hydrangeas fall into one of two categories: the lacecaps, with their sparser more open flowers and altogether more delicate appearance, and the hortensias, with their huge blowsy 'mop-heads'. 'Grandiflora' is one of the latter, though its flowers lack the coarseness of many varieties, and the individual florets that make up the 'mop' are more delicate. It has creamy white ball-like flower heads in late summer; these are scented and seem to stay on the plant for ever, almost drying in situ! It will reach 1.5m (5ft). Hortensias range in colour from red, through lilac, to palest pink and white. They need water in very dry weather – even the bigger specimens will appreciate a few gallons. Left alone, they spread gracefully. Grow them in a sunny or semi-shaded position.

Lonicera x purpusii

One of the shrubby honeysuckles, this plant bears no resemblance to its climbing cousins, apart from having strongly scented flowers. It's rather lax and twiggy, so needs stronger forms around it (try evergreen *Fatsia japonica* or *Sarcococca* with a carpet of early spring bulbs like crocuses and *Chionodoxa*), but it's worth including because of the creamy white, spicily fragrant flowers that appear on bare twigs from December to March, when little else is showing signs of life. For the best flush of winter flowers it needs a warm summer, and thrives in well-drained soil in sun or partial shade. Thin out old wood occasionally after flowering but forget about pruning to a tidy shape; the plant is naturally twiggy and will grow to 2m (6ft). Cut a few flowering twigs for the house – the scent is delicious.

Magnolia sieboldii

In spring/early summer this big deciduous shrub produces scented open white flowers 8–10cm (3–4in) across with brilliant striking crimson bosses. Originating from Japan and Korea, it will reach a height of 5.5m (18ft), so make sure you have enough space for it! It has broad, somewhat oval, leaves of fresh green, and is hardy down to -20°C (-4°F). Magnolias are known to prefer acid to neutral soils, although *M. sieboldii*, like *M. stellata* and *M. kobus*, are tolerant of alkaline soils, as long as they're moist. For dry alkaline soils, grow evergreen *M. grandiflora* and its cultivars. Mulch all of them in spring with leaf mould. *Magnolia sieboldii* likes a sunny aspect but is also happy in light shade. It is a graceful and elegant shrub – one for the discerning city gardener.

Rosa 'Iceberg'

I've included 'Iceberg' here because this white rose is a classic that has stood the test of time. It's a floribunda rose of tall to medium height that flowers profusely over a long season. You have to prune this one hard in spring as, like hybrid teas, floribundas flower on the current season's wood (shoots that have grown in the same season). In spring cut all the branches down to within 30cm (12in) of the ground to an outward-facing bud. This stimulates new growth that bears the flowers. 'Iceberg' is very hardy and resistant to many common diseases like black spot and rust. There is a climbing sport that grows up to 5m (16ft) and flowers almost continuously. When trained on the wall of a house, 'Iceberg' is a stunning showpiece in summer, but it has little scent.

Rosa 'Roseraie de l'Haÿ'

'Roseraie de l'Haÿ' is a beautiful, tough, superbly scented rose for a prime spot in your garden. It roots very deeply, so mature plants withstand drought well. Very vigorous in growth, with apple-green young leaves and darker green older ones, it sends up strong thorny stems to form an open shrub, 2.3m (7ft) tall, so it's best placed at the back of a border. The eye-catching flowers are single, in colours between deep pink and carmine-purple. The scent is triple 'Wow!' – on still warm days it will drift tantalisingly over the entire garden. It flowers in June and intermittently throughout summer. In late summer it produces bright red flattened rosehips. It's easy to grow, needs no pruning, other than for shape, and looks good in mixed cottage-garden-style borders, and as a specimen plant.

Rosa rugosa 'Alba'

Rugosa, or Japanese, roses are, indeed, very rugged – no overbred fussy hybrid teas here! No pruning necessary, either. They have some of the most potent scents of all roses. The scent is free and can perfume the air all around the plant and further, especially on warm damp days. With fabulous scent comes vigorous foliage, which turns yellow in autumn. It has good resistance to black spot and other pests, and produces colourful hips that last over winter. 'Alba' is a simply gorgeous rose and, if I had my way, every garden would grow it! The flowers on this beauty are pure white and come over a long period, followed by large orange autumn hips. The scent is almost edibly moreish! Give it some space – it'll grow to 2.3m (7ft) – and make sure you can get to it easily for a sniff! It also makes a good hedge.

Viburnum

The viburnums are a large group of medium-sized deciduous shrubs, many of which are highly scented. Some flower on bare stems in autumn/winter/early spring, while others flower in spring. Modest in appearance, they're invaluable as the supporting cast in the garden's structure. The flowers are usually white, tinged with pink, and generally in tight clusters. *V.* x *burkwoodii* (pictured) smells deliciously of cloves. Unchecked, it will grow to 2–3m (6–8ft). *Viburnum* x *bodnantense* 'Dawn' is clothed from autumn until spring with pink honey-scented flowers. Spring-flowering *V.* x *carlcephalum*, the fragrant snowball viburnum, has large globe-shaped flower heads some 13cm (5in) across, which are pinkish in bud and open to pure white, with a richly sweet scent. *Viburnum carlesii* and *V.* x *juddii* are similarly scented.

CLIMBERS • WALL SHRUBS

A garden without climbers is like flat-lining with plants. Climbers give you curtains, drapes and backdrops, cover a multitude of sins and create green screens of privacy in the middle of the city.

Plant up your walls and fences before you plant anything else. Where privacy is important, choose evergreens, such as *Clematis armandii* 'Apple Blossom', In areas enjoyed in summer, plant scented sweet peas, roses, honeysuckle and jasmine. Climbing plants are so adaptable. Train them over obelisks or willow wigwams to give that all-important vertical dimension to a border. Train them along a pergola until they cover the horizontals. Grow them through other plants (up trees and through hedges). Let them scramble, ramble or just do their own thing in wilder parts of the garden. And don't forget that what goes up can come down: you can let climbers trail if you wish!

THE KNOW-HOW

When choosing plants for vertical definition in the garden, it's important to find out *how* they climb first. Then you can match them to the appropriate support.

Suckers and aerial roots Climbers like Virginia creeper (*Parthenocissus quinquefolia*), ivy and climbing *Hydrangea petiolaris* require a solid surface such as a wall to adhere to and climb their way skyward. They're ideal for covering large areas as you won't need to provide additional support.

Tendrils Sweet peas (*Lathyrus*), *Clematis* and vines (*Vitis*) use tendrils or modified leaves to hook onto supports. Choose thin trellis or wire that they can wind around and attach themselves to securely.

Twiners Runner beans, honeysuckle, *Wisteria* and jasmine have stems that coil around any slender support as the tip of the stem heads for the light.

When all these climbers are small, they benefit from some help from the gardener in getting started, by guiding and gently tying-in the new growth. Some climbers will amaze you and romp away after just a nod in the right direction (runner beans and *Clematis montana*, for example), while others, like ivy, will dither for a while before making their first point of contact. We can cheat with roses, which don't produce their own climbing aids, by training and tying in the long stems over supports.

RIGHT SUPPORT, RIGHT PLANT!

Growing climbers has to be a perfect marriage of plant and support, otherwise you'll have a heap of tangly stems on the ground. Supports must be strong enough for the job as they will need to support a considerable amount of weight as the plant matures. Climbers tend to mature fast, and what you mustn't do is realise your mistake when the plant's become a monster, and your cane and string construction is falling down; think heavy-duty right from the start.

• Choose a big strong support to start with. Don't be deceived by the plant when it's a junior. Think sturdy supports made from wire or wood.

• Sweet peas can climb up a wigwam of ordinary garden canes if you weave string or pliable twigs spirally around the canes to give them something to grip onto. They'll also climb up rough string.

• Wisterias were made for pergolas – their fantastic lilac-coloured scented flowers hang down in absolute profusion!

Tendrils of a Passiflora

• Keep an eye on your climbers. Some stems will 'wander' from the supports, so tie them in with soft string. Check them regularly during the growing season.

• Use green or neutral string for tying in. Nothing looks worse than neon ties!

• Don't plant the roots right next to walls because the soil there is too dry. Plant 30cm (12in) or more away, and lean the plants back towards the wall. The quality of soil at the foot of walls is also poor, so enrich it well with compost.

• Climbers will quickly add structure and colour in a new garden while your immature shrubs and trees get going.

• City gardens are often small; vertical planting can double the usable space.

• Supports don't need to be in the 'cottagey willow' style. Go contemporary with stainless steel or galvanised metal to suit monochrome and minimalist designs.

Chaenomeles speciosa

The ornamental cousin of the culinary quince, *Chaenomeles speciosa* is a wall shrub that loves the shade of a north-facing wall. The deciduous thorny branching growth needs training to a support. Trained specimens should be cut back after flowering. Although very shade-tolerant, it produces a more lavish display of saucer-shaped flowers when grown in the sun. Flowers appear in early spring and are blood-red, orange, pink or white, as in 'Nivalis' (pictured). When they fade, large aromatic yellow-green quince fruit stay on the plant for a long time. 'Simonii' is a dwarf spreading variety with dark red semi-double flowers; 'Geisha Girl' is medium-sized with double deep apricot flowers. All like a well-drained soil and tolerate chalk.

Clematis armandii

This vigorous evergreen, which grows to 6m (20ft), has long oval glossy leaves, which look good all year, and winter/early spring flowers. It needs no pruning, other than to maintain size or manage untidiness; if you do need to trim it, do so immediately after flowering. Plant in good soil enriched with compost. The flowers are single, 5cm (2in) across, saucer-shaped and scented of vanilla or almonds. For better flowers, choose a named cultivar, such as 'Apple Blossom', with pink-tinged white flowers, or 'Snowdrift'. *Clematis armandii* is ideal as a fragrant option for a west- or southwest-facing wall in a sheltered courtyard, growing over a pergola or trained up wires along a wall. In cold winters frost can singe the leaves and they may droop, but don't worry, it'll recover by spring.

***Clematis* 'Niobe'**

This exotic large-flowered *Clematis* has single, rich deep red blooms with yellow anthers, each flower 10–15cm (4–6in) across. These appear from early to late summer, and sometimes in a second flush in autumn. It's not terribly vigorous, making it ideal for genteel trelliswork or training through trees and large shrubs like *Garrya elliptica* and *Forsythia*, which are otherwise dull plants throughout the summer. It needs 'in-between' pruning: nothing too severe – think of taking off a third. Don't prune the main shoots but shorten the side ones to a pair of buds, in late winter/early spring. Other favourites include 'Mrs N. Thompson', with violet flowers, and 'Marie Boisselot', with pure white flowers. All three like a south- or west-facing site and good moist soil, and grow 2–3m (6–10ft) high.

Clematis tangutica

This species of *Clematis* is the only one with yellow flowers. Originally from China, it has elegant grey-green leaves and lantern-shaped deep yellow flowers 4cm (2in) long, borne singly on 15cm (6in) stems. Flowering from August to October, silky fuzzy seed heads, resembling a bad hair-do, appear as the petals drop, and there are always both flowers and seed heads on the plant at the same time. *Clematis tangutica* flowers on growth made on the current season's wood, so prune it hard in late autumn/early spring: simply grab a handful of stems and cut to 30cm (12in) above ground level, above a set of healthy buds. The new spring growth will carry that year's flowers. 'Bill MacKenzie' is a good cultivar, suiting any aspect. It can reach 6m (20ft) grown through a large shrub.

Garrya elliptica

The silk tassel bush has evergreen leathery leaves, but its showpiece is really the stunning catkins that dangle in clusters from late winter onwards. On 'James Roof' these are silver-grey and 20cm (8in) long; on 'Evie' they are 30cm (12in) long – very dramatic and visually arresting! Both these plants are males; females produce round purple berries but their catkins are smaller. *Garrya* forms a dense upright shrub, or small tree, and is frost-hardy but can be half-hardy in some areas. Before planting in fertile well-drained soil, fix strong trellis or wires with vine eyes on a shady wall sheltered from cold winds (which *Garrya* loathes), and well away from frost pockets. After the catkins fade, grow bright annual climbers through the branches.

Hedera helix

Ivies make excellent groundcover and thrive in dry shade. They also free-climb (they don't need artificial supports). It's a mistake to think that ivy damages brickwork; worry only if the mortar is loose. Ivy is tough, but variegated ones prefer more sun and shelter from cold winds. 'Buttercup' (pictured) has pale green leaves in the shade, bright yellow in the sun, but don't give it a south-facing spot; if the sun's too hot, it will scorch. 'Goldheart' has leaves splashed with bright yellow; 'Goldchild' grey-green leaves with yellow margins; 'Sagittifolia Variegata' creamy white leaves. Expect small yellow blooms in autumn, followed by black fruits. Ivy can also be trained, used for topiary and grown in containers. It's ideal for small paved gardens, covering a large expanse of wall, fronted by pots of colourful flowers.

PLANT PROFILES CLIMBERS·WALL SHRUBS

***Humulus lupulus* 'Aureus'**
The golden hop is a hardy herbaceous twiner that dies back in winter but has a phenomenal rate of growth in spring/summer: it will grow 6m (20ft) in a season (must be on Viagra!), to cover a fence completely. In very early summer, lime-green shoots sporting bright golden yellow foliage spring up to twine over its supports. The 3cm (1in) spikes of slightly fragrant flowers appear in summer, followed by long pendant racemes of papery cones with a resinous scent. 'Aureus' likes a fertile soil and, for the best leaf colour, grow it in a sunny position on a west- or south-facing wall. Use it on a pergola to make a canopy, grow it with grapes or ivy, let it drape over an informal arbour or climb over arches – just simply chop off the dead stems in winter.

Hydrangea petiolaris
The Japanese climbing hydrangea makes a useful substitute for honeysuckle on a shady wall, although don't expect it to grow in really heavy shade. It stands up well to atmospheric pollution and thrives in industrial areas. With large dark heart-shaped green leaves, it's a slow-growing free climber, clinging to walls with aerial roots. In summer it bears frothy domed lace-cap-like flowers in creamy white, but it takes several years for the plant to reach flowering size. Give it some support until the aerial roots attach themselves, and ensure the soil is moist and fertile. In warm areas it can be semi-evergreen. It is best not planted against a painted exterior wall as you can't remove the climber for a repaint job! No spring pruning is needed, other than to maintain its shape.

Lathyrus latifolius
Everlasting pea is just the job for covering any eyesore in the garden. This scentless easy climbing pea can be trained over tree stumps, sheds, or what-have-you. It's an exuberant grower, climbing to 3m (10ft), with a number of named purple, red and pink forms that flower throughout summer. *Lathyrus latifolius* has pink-purple flowers; 'Albus' and 'White Pearl' speak for themselves. You'll need to provide support; netting, securely fixed, is adequate for it to cover dull walls and fences. It can fair zip along a chain-link fence! Try running it through a large host shrub, too, like *Cotinus*. It's not fussy about soil, and needs little attention. If it gets in the way, just chop off what you don't want, otherwise let it run. Pity about the lack of scent, but you get longevity instead.

Lonicera japonica

You would not be thanked for giving a citizen of the southern US this honeysuckle – there, it's a classified weed! Japanese honeysuckle is great for covering trees, walls (if grown on trellis) and pergolas. It will gobble up an ugly shed or stretch of chain-link fence, and makes up for any thuggishness by a sweet pervasive scent. The masses of white spring flowers turn buff-yellow in late summer. 'Halliana' (pictured) is a more profuse bloomer, flowering from an early age; var. *repens* has flowers touched with purple. More or less an evergreen with soft bright green leaves, *L. japonica* appreciates a warm garden, its roots in moist shade. It will grow to 9m (30ft); if it's too vigorous, hack it back in spring. It will need watering in dry spells, though older plants are more drought-tolerant.

Solanum jasminoides

From the same family as the potato and the aubergine, the potato vine loves full sun and a west-facing wall, and it needs to be tied in as summer progresses. A scrambling evergreen or semi-evergreen climber, it produces frothy masses of star-like flowers from late summer until the first frosts. Its leaves are narrow and shiny, and about 5cm (2in) long. The non-fragrant (this is a point of hot debate, but I can't smell any fragrance!) blue-white flowers are 3cm (1in) long with prominent yellow anthers, and are held in clusters that smother the plant. 'Album' (pictured) has pure white flowers. The more commonly seen *Solanum crispum*, otherwise known as the Chilean potato tree, is a climber with lilac-purple flowers; it looks like a lilac gone mad!

Trachelospermum jasminoides

Star, or confederate, jasmine hails from India to Japan, and is a twining woody evergreen climber. Its glossy deep green leaves turn bronze-red in winter, while from mid- to late summer pure white star-shaped flowers, 3cm (1in) across, give off a lovely sweet scent, especially when the air is still. It needs full sun/part-shade, and hates a windy situation; site it against a warm sunny south- or west-facing wall. It can also be grown successfully in a container, though you will need to provide support for the stems, which grow long enough to cover an arch; it also makes a good conservatory plant. Unusually for a variegated plant, the cultivar 'Variegatum' is hardier than the species, its leaves turning crimson-pink in winter. 'Wilsonii' has bronze leaves turning crimson with the cold.

£ 289.50

PERENNIALS

My young nephew understands 'herbaceous' perennials to be plants that 'disappear in winter and then come back again'. He's right: perennials can be quite long-lived, despite their top growth dying back for winter, and there are even a few evergreens whose leaves persist.

Although perennials are usually grown together as a group in borders, you can successfully intermix them with shrubs and bulbs, where they provide useful infill. In winter an all-perennial border will be bare, while in summer it will take centre stage. Site such borders carefully – not outside your living-room window if you want to see evidence of life in January! Tender perennials (pelargoniums and patio plants) are ideal for containers, while many perennials are suitable for cut flowers.

Perennials are ideal for keeping continuity of flowering in the garden, and they do this mainly from early spring to late autumn. There is a perennial for every soil and situation. You can grow many of them from seed, but nurseries and garden centres sell masses of plants quite cheaply. The best time to buy is when they're in flower, so you can see if you like the plant, although autumn and spring are traditional times for planting out. If you're short of cash, you can generally get away with buying one plant and splitting it into two or three – if not in the first spring, then definitely in the second. Oriental poppies and Japanese anemones can be propagated by root cuttings, and pinks, carnations and diascias from stem cuttings.

THE KNOW-HOW

Many perennials are shallow-rooting, so need watering in dry periods. Sprinkle fertiliser or compost around them in spring and gently hoe in. Most need to be lifted and divided every three to four years to maintain the plant's vigour. Dig the plant up and prise the roots apart with a fork (or even cut right through the roots with a knife) until you get two/three more plants, each with plenty of roots. Replant, water carefully and keep free from invasive weeds. Many perennials like *Heuchera*, *Tiarella*, lily of the valley and lamb's ears (*Stachys byzantina*) make excellent groundcover plants and need minimal maintenance. Tidy away dead foliage in autumn, mulch with compost in spring, and that's it!

If you like playing about with plant associations and colour, you'll find an inexhaustible resource with perennials – these are the plants that garden designers love.

• Plant spring-flowering bulbs around perennials as the bulbs will flower before the perennials get going, providing that vital early spring colour.

• Taller perennials (delphiniums, lupins) need staking. Put the stakes in position before the plants actually need them. Metal linking ones, or circles, are ideal, and they become hidden by the foliage as the plants grow through them.

Lilium regale

• Cottage gardens were full of perennials. Take a look at Gertrude Jekyll's designs and gardens, and be inspired!

• It's possible to have colour-themed gardens with perennials – think of the white garden at Sissinghurst. There are so many species with flowers in almost every colour, including green.

• Plant in groups of three, five, seven – even numbers somehow always look, well, rather odd!

• Give perennials plenty of space. In their second year they bulk up dramatically. You can always fill in gaps around them in the first year with annuals.

• Some perennials get too long and straggly early on. After the first flowering cut them down hard to the ground to encourage a bushier shape and, hopefully, a second flush of flowers.

Achillea filipendulina

Yarrow is an old garden favourite, introduced into Britain in the early 1800s; the white clustered flower heads of the wild form are often seen by the roadside. For the dry garden, achilleas are one of the most dependable tall perennials, tolerating city pollution well. *Achillea filipendulina* has bright yellow flowers, with 'Gold Plate' a recommended cultivar; it makes a clump of feathery dark green leaves 30cm (12in) high, from which strong stems emerge, some 1.2m (4ft) high, carrying the flowerheads that resemble chanterelle mushrooms. Each flower is made up of many tiny florets that look good from June to September. *Achillea* like well-drained soil in full sun. Space plants 60cm (2ft) apart; in exposed places they need staking. They make good dried flowers.

Anemone x hybrida

Japanese anemones make fine border plants from August to October, when many other plants have finished flowering. Delicate-looking but robust, they grow up to 1.5m (5ft) tall with long flower stems held high above lush vine-like leaves. They prefer a moisture-retentive soil in part-shade, but will also do well in full sun. The flowers are saucer-shaped and long-lasting, appearing in succession. 'Honorine Jobert' (pictured) has pure white flowers; 'Margarete', rose-pink, and 'Max Vogel' very light pink. These beauties associate well with Michaelmas daisies and *Ligularia*. Although they are said to hate disturbance, I know of specimens that have been lifted and divided, and still flowered the same year. Give them space as *A.* x *hybrida* cultivars will spread rapidly.

Asphodeline lutea

Jacob's rod likes to grow in hot sunny areas that never get waterlogged, preferring sandy, loamy, dry soil, and is ideal in a border or on a dry bank. This clump-forming, rather architectural, perennial has 35cm (14in) stems covered with narrow grassy blue-green leaves. Hugging the stems in late spring are bright yellow six-petalled star-shaped flowers; the overall effect is something like a patio flare. Later, seed pods form; these resemble green cherries but eventually turn brown. The more delicate and paler yellow *Asphodeline liburnica* comes into flower when *A. lutea* is forming seed pods. Grow them together for continuity and have flowers into late summer. *Asphodeline lutea* associates well with *Lysimachia* 'Firecracker', smaller euphorbias and scarlet-flowered *Geum* 'Mrs Bradshaw' or 'Red Wings'.

Cimicifuga simplex

Unfortunately, this purple-leaved Japanese native doesn't have a simple name! A clump-former, it flowers in late autumn, throwing up numerous 1.2m (4ft) stems with pink-tinged cream flowers; these sport prominent stamens that crowd together on a slender bottlebrush, reminding me of a wayward firework! It associates well with other purples like *Monarda* and *Verbena hastata*. After the flowers have faded come greenish-white, turning brown, star-shaped follicles (dry fruits). 'Brunette' has dark red-brown foliage and stems; 'Elstead' purple-tinted buds and white flowers. *Cimicifuga* are ideal for cool shady conditions, like a moist border, where you want a bit of drama! They prefer moist, free-draining soil but dislike too much sun, which will scorch their leaves.

Cirsium rivulare

Much loved at recent Chelsea Flower Shows, *Cirsium* are eye-catching central European natives and *de rigueur* in trendy gardens. Think of a thistle (but much more refined) with vivid ruby-red flowers some 3cm (1in) across, then take away the prickles. The flowers also come in purple, red or yellow. Many *Cirsium* are invasive, which is fine if you want a spreader because it's a cliché of a beautiful plant. Dead-head to prevent seeding. 'Atropurpureum' (pictured), which needs full sun, has deep crimson flower heads from early to midsummer, and grows to 1.2m (4ft) on strong stems. It partners well with grasses, especially *Miscanthus sinensis* and *Stipa*, and *Verbena hastata*. *Echinops* and *Eryngium giganteum* look good with it, too.

Echinacea

Ideal for prairie-style plantings, coneflowers are late-summer-flowering perennials from North America, where they were used by Native Americans to treat infections. Considering their height (1m/3ft), they're mean with their flowers, but this deficiency is offset by a long and late flowering season, from June to September. The flowers are 'all centre and floppy petals', as some put it – well, they are large, with a hard orange-brown central cone surrounded by a ring of long drooping petals, held high on stiff stems that have rough, toothed leaves. The flowers can be purple, red or pink, although 'August Corigia' (pictured) is cerise-purple; 'White Swan' speaks for itself. *Echinacea* love a deep well-drained soil rich in humus, in full sun, but ultimately they're not too fussy.

Lilium regale

Renowned for their powerful sweet scent, *Lilium regale* make majestic tall focal points wherever they're planted, reaching a height of 1.5m (5ft). Buy the biggest bulbs you can find. They do particularly well in large containers or in rich neutral-to-acid border soil. It's a stem-rooting lily, which means you must plant it deeply, some 10–20cm (4–8in) into the soil. It will send up vigorous fat stems, and in June some 25–30 outward-facing trumpet-shaped flowers will appear. These are white inside with a yellow throat, although *L. regale* 'Album' is pure white inside and out; there is also the yellow-flowered 'Royal Gold'. Watch out for lily beetle; inspect your lilies regularly for these voracious bright red creatures and their small slug-like larvae that eat away at the underside of leaves. Pick them off and squash!

Monarda

Bergamots are highly aromatic perennials, growing to 1m (3ft), with an exciting colour range. From midsummer to autumn, the tubular flower clusters can be white, pink, red or violet; the bracts are often coloured, too. These clusters sit around the main stem. As each one develops, another piece of stem grows from the middle of the flower, topped with a second smaller whorl. 'Beauty of Cobham' (pictured) has green leaves with a purple cast, and pale pink flowers with purple-pink bracts; 'Cambridge Scarlet' is brilliant scarlet; 'Loddon Crown' a dark-red purple; 'Schneewittchen' white. Bees love the nectar-rich flowers, and the dried leaves make herb tea. Bergamots need full sun/light shade and soil that doesn't dry out in summer. The stems and foliage need cutting down to ground level in autumn.

Physostegia virginiana

How nice to have a plant you can boss around! The obedient plant, as *Physostegia* is commonly known, is beloved of flower arrangers because the small individual snapdragon-like flowers have hinged stalks that can be moved into a new position – where they obligingly stay. Flowering from June to September, this North American native can be a rather rampant customer, spreading by rhizomes to clumps several metres across. The flowers are purple, pink or white, like 'Summer Snow', which grows to 45–60cm (1½–2ft). 'Summer Spire' has deep lilac-purple flowers; 'Vivid' is a deep pink. *Physostegia* need light shade and a moisture-retentive soil. Mulch and water well during very dry spells, and cut them down to ground level in autumn.

Pimpinella major

The Latin name of this plant always makes me think of... well, the seedier side of life, but see if you can find an easier way of remembering it. Whether Gran would have approved of my connotations or not, she would certainly have felt most at home with this 1–1.2m (3–4ft) cow parsley look-alike – except that it's pink. Ah, but *Pimpinella* also come in white, yellow and purple, the flowers followed by round fruits. These are plants for naturalising in those 'I-didn't-know-I-planted-it-there' wild gardens, but don't plant them singly – they'll look silly. Go for companies of threes or fives, in sun or part-shade. Any soil suits, as long as it's moist. You get double value with 'Rosea' (pictured) because it has pale pink and deep pink flowers on the plant at the same time, in early to midsummer.

Polygonatum x hybridum

The curious common name Solomon's seal refers to the rounded seal-like scars on the rhizomes, and to the plant's supposed ability to seal wounds! Its graceful arching wands are seen in late spring/early summer. The 1m (3ft) stems have paired upward-curving leaves along their length, followed by small dangling creamy white bellflowers, which look a little like snowdrops. The whole habit of this plant is subtle and distinctive. *Polygonatum odoratum* flowers at a similar time, with tubular green-tipped bellflowers that are delicately scented. These are followed by round black fruit. Its cultivar 'Flore Pleno' has double flowers; 'Gilt Edge' has leaves with yellow margins. Solomon's seal does well in any soil and likes shade; too much sun will scorch its tender leaves badly.

Verbena bonariensis

This classy late-summer statement in the back of the border, with its 2m (6ft) vertical stems, towers above other plants, but despite its height, it carries itself gracefully. Small lavender-purple flowers, which are very long-lasting, branch out along the main stem, ending in a final iridescent cluster. The thin, square, wiry stems splay out in all directions. Although they don't look terribly wind-resistant, they are quite robust but may need staking in exposed situations. You can grow them from seed, which is useful because plants can be expensive, but small plants need cosseting through their first winter. If it's cold and wet, they will not do well, so planting them in well-drained soil with some protection is beneficial. Place them close together in a clump about 10cm (4in) apart for best effect.

GROUNDCOVER • GRASSES

I've put these two groups of plants together for one reason: generally, they are both easy to maintain.

GROUNDCOVER

This is a word that never excites much interest, but groundcover plants are a great solution for those difficult areas where nothing much will grow (such as the dry shade under trees or against walls) or for those parts of the garden that we haven't got the energy or creativity to deal with right now (such as inaccessible places like steep slopes). This is where the type of plant that looks okay, does the job and doesn't require much in the way of maintenance really comes into its own.

Whereas groundcover plants were long deposed to the realm of the uninspiring or just plain boring, in recent years they have burst out of the shadows. Sure, they'll never be centre stage but you don't want them to be. We want them to be dependable and do the job, but it would be nice if they could add interest and give a few surprises, too.

Well, many groundcover plants are ornamental in their own right, like hostas, *Lamium* 'Beacon Silver' and the red-splashed *Houttuynia cordata* 'Chameleon'. For permanent, almost zero-maintenance on slopes, plant *Cotoneaster dammeri*, *Hypericum calycinum* or *Juniperus squamata* 'Blue Star'. Thymes make good groundcover in hot spots, as do lavenders and rosemary planted close together and, of course, ivies do the same for dense tree shade.

GRASSES

One of the problems with grasses isn't the plants themselves, it's the name! By long association we've come to think of grass as meaning lawns, golf courses or fields… and with that goes the nagging adjunct: grass means work. And it's boring. And it's everywhere. So why make a big fuss about it?

I know, I know. A lot of you are thinking, 'Why should I plant grass?' But there's grass, and there's grass… The kind I'm talking about is nothing like the stuff you cut every week in summer – I'm talking fancy stuff, here! Ornamental grasses come in all sizes and forms, and bring a delicate touch to the border. Tall grasses move in the breeze, they look great in evening light. Some, like *Stipa gigantea* are huge, yet they never overpower or smother other plants. We should learn about them and use them more often. Grasses make ideal 'fillers' between plants in the herbaceous border, or, carefully placed, their upright arching form is accentuated when interplanted among shrubs. They don't scream for attention, yet their presence is soothing. And they were made for dry 'river-bed' planting schemes where decorative gravel is the main feature.

• Essentially, groundcover means 'plant and forget' – the ideal solution for busy city folk and also for the front of a border, especially if you're planting in tiers.

• Although groundcover plants and grasses are tough, make sure you pick the right ones for the right location (as always!).

• For the least work, choose evergreens for groundcover, such as the ultra-tough *Cotoneaster microphyllus* and ivy.

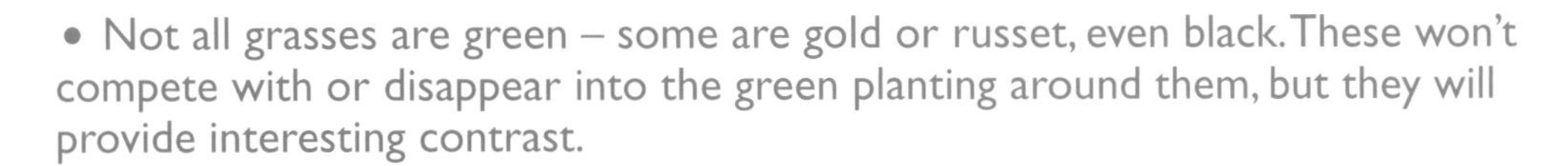

• Not all grasses are green – some are gold or russet, even black. These won't compete with or disappear into the green planting around them, but they will provide interesting contrast.

• The seed heads on most grasses go on for ever, some lasting right through winter. The taller ones move beautifully in the wind.

• Grasses are easy to grow. They don't need fertiliser, and most need no extra watering – excellent for the gardener who has little time.

• Treat most grasses like herbaceous perennials. As the clumps slowly increase, outgrowing their allocated space, divide them in spring.

• Evergreen grasses like *Carex buchananii* and *Festuca glauca* can be left untouched all year round. Just comb them through with your hand to remove any dead leaves.

• Cut herbaceous grasses like *Miscanthus sacchariflorus* down to 30cm (12in) each spring to help encourage a new crop of lush leaves.

Brunnera macrophylla

For dappled shade in woodland areas or among early spring flowerers, *Brunnera macrophylla* is a delicate-leaved perennial that spreads by means of rhizomes. It's not a dominant plant and brings a light touch wherever it's used. With softly hairy, almost heart-shaped, green leaves 5–20cm (2–8in) long on slender leaf stalks, it grows no more than 45cm (18in) tall, and that includes the flowers. These appear from mid- to late spring and are bright blue, reminiscent of forget-me-nots in both colour and form. Good cultivars are 'Hadspen Cream', with creamy white leaf margins; 'Langtrees', with spotted leaves; and 'Betty Bowring', which bears white flowers. It likes humus-rich moist soil that's also well drained. What it does not care for is sun, which will quickly crisp its large leaves.

Carex buchananii

We're into bog-country here with the sedges. To most of us they look like boggy field grasses, and so they're often overlooked. Yet in the garden their colourful or variegated leaves can act as foils for other more spectacular plants. And there's a sedge for practically every situation. In particular, they are useful for damp areas. *Carex buchananii*, the leatherleaf sedge, will grow in virtually any spot in sun or partial shade, as long as the soil doesn't veer into the extremes of very dry or very wet. And being so well behaved, sedges are ideal for containers. This one has rich reddish-brown leaves with curled leaf tips that arch upwards and outwards in a vase shape. Brown flowering spikes, 1m (3ft) long, appear in summer. Sedges look particularly good against stone and brickwork.

Cornus canadensis

A member of the dogwood family grown for its colourful stems and autumn leaves, this is known as the creeping dogwood, a perennial that colonises the ground by rhizomes. Its 3–4cm (1–1½in) long, oval leaves are attractive, arranged in overlapping circles. In late spring and early summer, green flowers surrounded by white, sometimes pink, bracts sit in the middle of the leaves, and last some time. The flowers are followed by round red fruit. With a height of no more than 15cm (6in), this modest spreader will do well in a soil that's on the acid side, and it also likes the shade, making it ideal for growing under camellias and rhododendrons. A clump of pale pink *Cyclamen hederifolium*, flowering in mid- to late autumn, would add interest when the dogwood's flowers are over.

Festuca glauca
You'll probably spot this grass in the nursery above all others as it really does stand out. Most perennial *Festuca* are grown for their leaves, which are usually a striking blue-green or blue-grey. They grow in a tuft, a fierce little clump of spiky-looking narrow leaves about 30cm (12in) tall – no blue-rinse brigade here, though the shape of the plant does resemble an exploded bun of the hair variety! The blue is an odd, almost surreal, colour for a grass, and is particularly at home in contemporary container schemes or minimalist gardens featuring glass or metal. *Festuca glauca* is evergreen; 'Harz' has blue-green leaves tipped with purple; 'Blaufuchs' has bright blue leaves. But for the best colour, choose 'Elijah Blue' (pictured), and contrast it against simple pea gravel so it really stands out.

***Lysimachia nummularia* 'Aurea'**
Once creeping Jenny is in your garden, you probably won't be able to get rid of it, but don't worry – this plant is easy on the eye and so obliging that you won't begrudge its presence. It spreads quickly, sending leafy stems along the ground until whole areas are covered by a golden yellow mat of 2cm (¾in) leaves. In summer it produces little upturned cup-shaped yellow flowers. Although an evergreen perennial, it will die back in severe winters, but some part always survives to reappear in spring. 'Aurea' is a great softener, adding a touch of randomness and informality to new gardens, especially when it trails over concrete steps; it can also be grown in hanging baskets. It likes moist soil, doing well around ponds and boggy areas, but is not so happy in full sun.

Miscanthus
Grown for their flowers, seed heads and variegated leaves, *Miscanthus* are tall grasses, ideal for the back of a border. They all prefer a sunny spot and free-draining soil. *Miscanthus sinensis* 'Dixieland' is one of the loveliest variegated forms, with wide yellow- and green-striped leaves, but it's also a bit of a whopper, whereas 'Morning Light', with its grey-green-and-white-striped leaves, reaches a height and spread of only 1.2m (4ft). Choose *M. sinensis* for oatmeal-coloured flowers or 'Flamingo' (pictured), my favourite, for its subtly pink-tinged flowers. *Miscanthus sacchariflorus* is a vigorous beast, reaching 3m (10ft). *Miscanthus* benefit from being cut back hard each spring, but don't be too eager to remove dead flower heads – they look magical in winter, especially when encrusted in an early morning frost.

***Ophiopogon planiscapus* 'Nigrescens'**
A horticultural oddity like no other, *O. planiscapus* 'Nigrescens' is straight from the Addam's Family garden. Commonly known as black grass, it is actually a member of the lily family. Racemes of white flowers dangle above the foliage in early summer and are followed by deep blue/black berries. The leaves resemble a plush feather boa but they belie the plant's true character: black grass is a tough all-rounder that thrives in sun or shade, and grows in most free-draining soils. Only 15cm (6in) tall, 'Nigrescens' is the perfect groundcover for the front of a border, a foil for showy alpines, or combine it with snowdrops for a bold minimalist look in a contemporary container. As it doesn't take up much space, repeat it throughout the garden to add a sense of rhythm to your planting.

Panicum virgatum
Known as deer tongue grass (presumably because it resembles a deer's tongue!), this US native grows naturally in many varied habitats but prefers damp soil. *Panicum* is suited to prairie-style plantings or gravel gardens, where its subtle autumn tints are seen to best advantage, and it does best planted in drifts so the plants can support each other. *Panicum virgatum* has glaucous-green stems and flat leaves with airy panicles of tiny purple-green flowers. 'Rehbraun' (pictured) and 'Hänse Herms' (fountain-like habit and reddish-purple autumn colour) are named after stolid German individuals, while 'Heavy Metal' (blue-grey leaves turning yellow in autumn) is an obvious favourite with the biking fraternity! *Panicum* thrive in poor soils, so there's no need to feed too often.

Pennisetum
These are a real favourite in the late season border. In September they drip with long cylindrical panicles of purple or burgundy flowers, which last well into winter. Most plants don't grow more than 1m (3ft), and being tidy and non-invasive, they're ideal for the small city garden. *Pennisetum setaceum* 'Rubrum' (pictured), the purple fountain grass, is the most dramatic, and works wonderfully with other late summer-flowering perennials like *Agapanthus*, *Rudbeckia* 'Herbstsonne' and purple *Echinacea*. Complement it with silver-leaved *Cerastium tomentosum*, or allow its feathery flowers, which resemble fluffy cats' tails, to soften bold architectural plants like *Phormium tenax*. Grow *Pennisetum* in a sunny position; too much shade causes both the flowers and leaves to fade, muddying the overall effect.

Stachys

The common names of this Mediterranean perennial are lamb's tongue and lamb's ears. It's a touchy-feely plant that children (and adults) adore; it's so soft and fleecy-looking, you just want to bend down and stroke it! The aptly named *S. byzantina* 'Silver Carpet' covers the ground in a dense mat of downy silver leaves. In light soil and full sun it will spread via horizontal stems. The 10cm (4in) long leaves persist over winter, although the plant will look a bit sad in very wet weather. Other cultivars like 'Big Ears' have purple flowers, as does *S. macrantha* 'Superba' (pictured). *Stachys byzantina* 'Cotton Boll' has little woolly balls along its stem. *Stachys* associates prettily with pinks, roses, catmint, irises and purple-leaved sage, but its uses are many, and it will never look out of place filling any gaps in a sunny border.

Stipa calamagrostis

Although there are some giants in this genus of feather grasses, there are others with a little more self-control! It's almost an insult to call *S. calamagrostis* a grass because it has as much ornamental value in the architectural department as any shrub. A deciduous perennial clump of arching fine green leaves in summer, it throws up tall stems with ultra-feathery silver/purple-tinted plumes, each flower spike nodding in the slightest breeze. Most people are familiar with Big Daddy *S. gigantea*, which grows to 2.5m (8ft) and has oat-like flowers; *S. calamagrostis* is its daintier cousin, with an overall height of 1.2m (4ft) and flower spikes 80cm (32in) long. There's always a place for a plant that has height without heaviness, so *S. calamagrostis* complements weighty evergreens perfectly.

Symphytum

Comfreys are invasive spreaders, tough and tolerant of dry shade. Often seen growing at the roadside in spring, they have large, 25cm (10in) long, coarse roughly oval leaves and hairy stems. Their 2cm (¾in) long flowers, which can be white, pinky-purple or mauve, appear from late spring to midsummer. *Symphytum officinale*, which grows to 1.5m (5ft), is also known as boneset or knitbone, and is used in herbal medicine. The white comfrey, *Symphytum orientale* (pictured), is smaller, growing to a height of 70cm (28in). Comfrey makes rapid groundcover and is ideal for the wild garden. If it gets too vigorous, chop it down and make fertiliser from the mineral-rich leaves. Alternatively, add the leaves to the compost heap or dig them into the soil when planting nutrition-lovers like roses.

ANNUALS • BIENNIALS

Often overlooked, these short-lived members of the plant world have a useful role to play in your garden. Don't pass them by simply because you think they're one-season wonders – they're not! They're a mass of colourful film extras waiting in the wings to fill the stage, plug the gaps or provide side-shows to the main event. They can be stars in their own right, too.

Annuals grow, flower and die within one year, whereas biennials take two years to complete their lifecycle, producing leaves in the first year, followed by flowers and seed in the second. Tender perennials are plants used as annuals (that is, they are replaced every year) because they dislike our cold climate in winter.

In a new garden, annuals and biennials fill the bare earth between small shrubs and perennials that haven't yet reached their full size, drawing them together, making the whole garden look more established. Always plant them in large groups because they just don't look good planted individually; they need each other's company for support and to create fabulous colour en masse. They're also useful in containers, hanging baskets and window boxes, where bold intense colour is needed. Hardy annuals, half-hardy annuals and tender perennials all have different requirements.

THE LOW DOWN...

Sow frost-hardy annuals in spring, directly into the ground where you want them to flower. If you're sowing seeds in the soil, wait until April or May, when the soil is nice and warm. Make sure you have a fine tilth of soil, then rake it smooth and level. Hardy annuals aren't fussy about soil, though most like full sun. Sow them thinly in shallow circular/meandering drills (lines). Mark the ends of each line with a stick to make weeding easier. If the emerging seedlings are too crowded, thin them out ruthlessly! The space between plants should eventually be about 15cm (6in). Half-hardy annuals need to be sown indoors and planted out only after all danger of frost is past.

Sow biennials in trays or in a seedbed in summer – unfortunately the time when most of us fancy lazing in our gardens! – and transplant them to their final positions in autumn. For long-lasting flowers in early spring right through to summer, biennials have the edge and give a fabulous display before the annuals arrive. If you like your garden to look at its best in spring, biennials fit the bill. They can look sad during the winter, though, but they're raring to go once the weather warms up.

Caring for annuals and biennials is easy. Water seedlings, thin ruthlessly, and pinch off dead flowers to encourage more. And just watch them flower! What's more, seeds are cheap, so you get a lot of plants for your money!

• You can sow annuals in modules: put a pinch of seed in each unit/pot, then plant the lot out in a clump when the plants are about 5cm (2in) high.

• Try to plant annuals and biennials in a sheltered spot, otherwise the wind will flatten the stems and you'll end up with an untidy display.

• Bedding plants are annuals. If you don't want to grow your own from seed, buy plug-plants from garden centres and pot them on. Remember that most plug-plants are half-hardy annuals, which can't stand frost.

Dianthus chinensis 'Strawberry Parfait'

• As summer progresses, you may need to provide support (sticks, twigs, etc.) and tie-in the plants loosely as they grow tall and floppy.

• A little fertiliser is fine, but too much will give you green sappy growth at the expense of the flowers.

• If the plants are healthy when planted out, they shouldn't be troubled by pests and diseases. To stop annuals and biennials becoming stressed and susceptible to disease, keep them well watered.

• Climbing annuals like *Ipomoea tricolor* 'Heavenly Blue' and *Thunbergia alata* (black-eyed Susan) are ideal for enlivening dull evergreens in summer.

Angelica gigas

The angelicas are all statuesque biennials, reaching 2.5m (8ft). Their tall ribbed hollow stems burst into heads of football-sized flower clusters resembling giant cow parsley. The common *Angelica archangelica* – all mid-green with green flower clusters – is used as a culinary herb, the stems in particular. *Angelica gigas* (pictured), on the other hand, has claret-red flowers and green foliage on purple stems, making a striking architectural statement. Is this plant a hardy biennial or a perennial? It certainly seeds itself with abandon and, as the seedlings germinate rapidly near the main stem, the plant will reappear next year in the same spot. The main plant may survive, too. It likes full sun or part-shade, and looks fantastic beside water or as a towering statement in the border.

Cleome hassleriana

You might think that the dramatic spider flower couldn't possibly be an annual: its height (60cm/2ft) and bushy habit suggest that it's longer-lived. It is, however, a fast-growing half-hardy annual that likes a sunny spot in a fertile well-drained soil. Given those conditions, it will shoot up, the flowers erupting in summer into fantastic pink narrow-petalled clusters with long protruding stamens – rather like an OTT pink firework! The flowers come in pink, purple, mauve or white. This plant has a dual character: you can grow it in the cottage garden or, because of its brazenly modern looks, you can site it in a dramatic contemporary design where its 'notice-me!' fine feathers will cut a dash among other strong architectural forms. Think element of surprise, think *Cleome*. It deserves to be more widely grown.

Dianthus barbatus

Biennial sweet William, which reaches 50–70cm (20–28in), is a traditional cottage-garden flower, invaluable in late spring/early summer bedding schemes. The flowers are borne in large heads on stout stems, and can be single or double. Colours range from magenta, rose, mauve, red and lilac to white, and many have a pronounced 'eye'. Modern strains have little scent, but the older ones have a wonderful fragrance, reminiscent of cloves. Seed can be sown as early as spring, but you can also sow the seed in trays or a seedbed in summer, and transplant the young plants to their final positions in autumn. Plant them about 15cm (6in) apart. Ordinary soil, even heavy clay, suits them, but they do like sun and survive dry weather without worry. The flowers last a long time and are excellent for cutting.

Digitalis purpurea
From the common foxglove comes the important heart drug digitoxin, and all species of *Digitalis* are poisonous. They are grown for their elegant spires of flowers, which may reach 1.5m (5ft). Foxgloves have an eye-catching shape and look best en masse in an informal setting. *Digitalis purpurea* is a fully hardy biennial, often grown as an annual. In late spring/summer tall spikes of flowers arise from its rosette of rough green leaves. The tubular flowers with their distinctive lip can be red, pink and white, as well as purple. Although foxgloves will grow in dry exposed conditions, they prefer shadier damper sites and a well-drained but moist soil. Where you need vertical accents to bring balance to a mainly horizontal planting, the foxglove will add a robust yet well-mannered touch.

Ipomoea tricolor
Morning glories are perennial climbers with spectacular saucer-shaped flowers, and are usually grown as annuals because they're not frost-hardy. 'Crimson Rambler' (pictured) has deep red flowers with a white throat, while 'Heavenly Blue' has sky-blue flowers, also with a white throat. Grow them against a very sheltered wall with some support, as they hate the wind. All can grow to 6m (20ft) in a season, so *Ipomoea* are ideal for some temporary screening. If you only get to enjoy your garden in the evening, or you entertain outside a lot in the summer, grow *I. alba*, the moonflower. Its huge white saucer-like flowers open at dusk, only to fade after sunrise. It has a luscious heady fragrance that will literally fill the entire garden; it'll make you want to sleep outside!

Isatis tinctoria
Otherwise known as woad, this is the plant the Anglo-Saxons used to ferment to get the blue dye for painting their faces and bodies in preparation for battle. Once a wild native, woad is now used in many wild garden designs. Numerous small yellow-petalled flowers are borne on tall grey-green stems. These fade to form wonderful pendent deep brown seed heads shaped like slippers, which hang down in bunches and persist on the plant for some time. Woad likes rich well-drained soil in full sun, but ordinary garden soil in good heart will do just fine. A hardy biennial, it self-seeds readily, and large ornamental grey-green rosettes will pop up everywhere. It doesn't thrive if it's grown in the same spot for more than two years, so sow it once and let it do the rest! It will grow to 60cm (2ft).

Lathyrus odoratus

Sweet peas always conjure pictures of dreamy cottage gardens, but that doesn't mean they can't be contemporary, too! These hardy annual climbers, growing to 2.5m (8ft), are renowned for their sweet scent, and make excellent cut flowers. Flower colour ranges from pastels to deep purples and reds. Older varieties usually have smaller flowers, but their scent is the sweetest, especially 'Matucana' and 'Painted Lady'. Support is essential; gently tie in the plants to wigwams of canes in early summer when they start to climb. Sow seed in pots from autumn to late winter before planting out in spring. They like sun, rich soil and plenty of water. Nip off the flowers as they fade to prolong flowering. 'Red Arrow' (pictured) has scarlet blooms that are not bleached by strong sun.

Myosotis sylvatica

Calling this plant 'forget-me-not' seems strange, since it's a common hardy biennial that pops up all over the place, making it impossible to forget, let alone get rid of! Lazy cottage gardeners love it. Once sown, it will self-seed like it's on steroids; all you have to do is move the seedlings wherever you want them... Or let them stay: in spring random drifts of this plant uncannily appear where they look utterly charming and make rapid groundcover, reaching a height of 15–30cm (6–12in). Generous drifts of its tiny blue flowers work well among spring bulbs. One of the best associations I've seen is yellow cottage tulips growing through a patch of sky-blue forget-me-nots. Easy as pie and as useful as could be, forget-me-nots may be old-fashioned but they're still a front-runner.

Nicotiana x sanderae

Grown as annuals in this country, *Nicotiana* x *sanderae*, with their trumpet-shaped flowers, are used exclusively as summer bedding plants. Known as tobacco plants, most bedding nicotianas come in pastel shades of red, white, lime-green, pink and purple. Cultivars in the Domino series (pictured) reach a height of 30–45 cm (12–18in), while those in the Starship series grow to a similar height but tolerate nasty weather better. Cultivars in the Merlin series are dwarf, growing to 20–25cm (8–10in) high, so are ideal for containers. For heady jasmine-like scent, try 'Evening Fragrance', 1m (3ft) high, or 'Fragrant Cloud', 60cm (2ft) high. They'll need staking and a fertile well-drained soil in a sunny position to do well, but on still August nights the scent is intoxicating.

Nigella damascena

Love-in-a-mist, or devil-in-a-bush, is a fast-growing upright hardy annual, 60cm (2ft) tall, with bright green feathery foliage. En masse, it looks as though the flowers are held in a green haze. A typical cottage-garden plant, its flowers can be sky-blue, deep blue, rose and white. Big drifts of the blue 'Miss Jekyll' look stunning, while 'Persian Jewels' provides a mix of colours. Very easy to grow and tolerant of most soil types, it's a favourite for children's gardens, being as tough as the proverbial old boot! Dead-head the flowers unless you want the highly decorative seed pods (the devil-in-a-bush part!). Large and inflated like oval balloons, these slowly change colour as summer slips into autumn, when they can be cut and dried for use in flower arrangements. Love-in-a-mist self-seeds like mad.

Papaver nudicaule

The Iceland poppy can be a short-lived perennial, biennial or an annual – it can't make up its mind. If conditions suit, it will stay around for longer than a season but as it self-seeds so promiscuously, it doesn't matter! Most poppies love full sun, and this is no exception, though it will also be happy in partial shade. There are many different varieties available with a wonderful range of colours, including red, orange, white and even salmon-pink! 'Summer Breeze' lasts for ages, growing to 30cm (12in). 'Garden Gnome' is dwarf, growing to half that size. Part of their beauty lies in the texture of the petals, which seem as fragile and thin as tissue paper, yet the plant is surprisingly robust and wind-resistant. It will bloom continuously throughout summer.

Ricinus communis

As a dramatic addition to a summer bedding scheme, the castor oil plant (the seeds produce castor oil, surprise, surprise!) is a real eye-catcher! A perennial grown as a half-hardy annual, it needs sowing under cover, then planting out in a sunny spot in well-drained soil when there's no danger of frost. *Ricinus communis* somewhat resembles a large-leaved houseplant: its leaves are 30cm (12in) across, shaped like a hand, and carried on sturdy stalks that branch from the main stem. Most castor oil plants are rich green, but 'Impala' is red-purple, and 'Zanzibariensis' green with conspicuous pale midribs. Both make dramatic focal points. It can grow to 1.5m (5ft), with a 1m (3ft) spread, and needs a lot of water. Not a plant for the child-friendly garden, though – all parts are deadly.

CONTAINER PLANTS

Growing plants in containers isn't the poor man's substitute for having a garden – it's a creative way of using plants in areas where there is no soil, and it's ideal for the gardener who likes to move his/her plants about! So don't feel left out if you have no 'garden'. You do – the only difference is that you aren't planting directly into Mother Earth.

Containers give you more scope than you might imagine; small trees do perfectly well in large pots, as do decorative vegetables. Containers focus the mind nicely, from deciding on solo specimens to which plant combinations work best – and it's all done on a small scale, so it's less work and less expensive, unless you get hooked on pots! Imagine a container as a picture frame. You stand back, decide what will suit the frame – which might be a terracotta pot, galvanised pail or rustic half-barrel – and carefully select your plants. Some of the most striking gardens are composed in containers.

If you have alkaline soil, then containers are the only realistic way to grow acid-loving plants like *Rhododendron* and *Camellia*. Also, if you want to grow bog plants, you can fashion your own mini-bog in a pot. With the right soil for the plant, you can grow whatever plants you fancy, even though they would sulk in your borders! Containers are great for people in wheelchairs because they bring both soil and plant to an easily workable height.

A NOTE ABOUT COMPOST

For permanent container plantings of trees, shrubs and perennials, always use a sterilised soil-based compost, like John Innes No 3, which holds onto water and nutrients well while encouraging good air movement and drainage. Soilless composts, which are usually peat-based, are lighter and easier to handle, but they don't have the same staying power as J. I. No 3, so they are typically used only for temporary or short-term plantings like hanging baskets, which are replaced every year. Peat-based composts are well aerated and moisture-retentive but they don't hold onto nutrients easily, which means that plants need feeding regularly throughout the growing season. Peat-free multipurpose composts are an environmentally friendly alternative and just as effective, but, again, they do need regular feeding. To replenish the nutrients in composts the easy way, sprinkle some controlled-release fertiliser like 'Osmocote' over the surface. It'll say exactly how much and how often on the packet.

You can make your own composts. For my containers, I like to use half J. I. No 3 and half peat-free multipurpose – the best of both worlds. But you could add lots of homemade garden compost and leaf mould if your chosen plants need a humus-rich soil. For plants that need extra-free-draining soil, like alpines, use lots of horticultural grit.

• You can use virtually anything as a plant container: large olive oil cans, wine crates, rusty watering cans, metal saucepans, wheelbarrows, even old wellies.

• Terracotta pots that aren't guaranteed frost-free are likely to crumble, crack, flake or fall to pieces.

• Make sure all containers have drainage holes. If they don't, drill them yourself using the appropriate drill bit.

• Raise all terracotta containers off the ground in hard winters (use pot feet), otherwise the bottoms might freeze and fall off.

• 'Crocks' at the bottom of the pot aren't always necessary unless the plant demands good drainage. If it does, use bits of broken terracotta, gravel or even small pieces of polystrene where weight is an issue.

• If the pot is likely to blow over, anchor it to the ground before planting it up. Drill a hole in the pot and poke a small stake through it into the soil. If the pot is to stand on concrete, drill a hole and put a long screw into a rawl-plug.

• When planting up terracotta pots, water the plants in well, as the unglazed pottery itself will soak up a lot of the water.

• Container gardens move house with you!

• There's no heavy digging or hoeing involved, just pulling out the odd weed.

• Containers need regular watering in summer, perhaps every day. Get an automated drip-feed system if you're too busy to do it.

• Choose plants to cascade over the edge of containers, as well as for the centre.

PLANT PROFILES CONTAINER PLANTS

Agapanthus
These African lilies are bulbous, clump-forming perennials, providing a striking display of ball-shaped 13cm (5in) flower clusters late in the summer. They're sun-lovers, so position them somewhere sheltered, and fully hardy to half-hardy. In the garden they need a good soil and lots of water. In autumn, cut the foliage back. Most *Agapanthus* are blue, like 'Blue Giant', but there are some white cultivars, such as 'Albus' (pictured) and 'Bressingham White', which look particularly dramatic in the evening. The flowers are borne on tall stems 60–100cm (2–3ft) high, which rise above arching strap-shaped leaves. For container-growing, choose a large deep pot to accommodate their roots. They really are plants to grow by themselves in a pot; there isn't room for much else!

Buxus sempervirens
This is the gardener's equivalent of kid's play-putty, except you use clippers, not your hands, to shape it! Small dark green evergreen leaves and a dense habit characterise it – but apart from that, it's what you make it! Box is happy in sun or semi-shade; it'll make a hedge 2m (6ft) high or 20cm (8in) high – you can take clippers to it quite viciously, and it won't complain. But a little more care will reward you handsomely. Feed and water it in spring/summer and growth will be more lush. Box balls or pyramids in terracotta pots are a cliché – but what a nice one! – and a topiary frame over a young plant can give you a cat, swan or whatever. Box plants are expensive and relatively slow-growing, but they are so amenable and give such a calm focused effect, alone or in groups, that they're a must.

Canna
This exotic-looking perennial bears vivid punchy flowers on tall stems in late summer. Growing to 1.5m (5ft), it's a favourite of municipal bedding schemes and roundabout planting, but you'll appreciate it better as a container plant on your own patch. The flowers bawl colour: scarlet with 'President', scarlet-edged yellow with 'Lucifer', golden yellow with 'King Midas', as well as in-between shades of red and orange. The flowers look a bit like gladioli, but the plants are stouter, and the leaves more lush and *Hosta*-like. *Canna* need loads of humus, and they do well in large pots in a sheltered sunny position. They die back with the first frost, and thereafter you should keep them frost-free. Simply take the container inside, or lift the rhizomes and store them in a cool dry place.

Convallaria majalis

Lily of the valley is a small wee thing that sometimes 'disappears' in the garden, and its extremely fragrant flowers are a long way below nose-reach, but growing it in a container means that you can tailor-make the soil and site, as well as make the plants more accessible. This perennial rises from a spreading rhizome. Its almost elliptical 5–20cm (2–8in) long leaves can be striped, as in 'Albostriata', or dark green. Arching stems bear the nodding white bellflowers; several hang loosely on each stem. The scent is intense! A container of lily of the valley looks fabulous as a lone centrepiece on a garden table, or you could mix them with small ferns, anemones, fritillarias, grape hyacinths and *Corydalis* for a fresh spring flavour. It likes leaf mould and moist soil in full sun/part shade.

Cordyline australis

For year-round interest, the cabbage tree (don't worry, it doesn't look like a cabbage) is a bit of a sparkler! With palm-like leaves that shoot up in a fan shape, it's similar in appearance to a phormium. In containers, cordylines will grow to about 3m (10ft). They like full sun and will survive drought as mature specimens, though you should water them freely when they're young, and feed in spring and summer. Sheltered south-facing walls should provide adequate winter protection. Dead leaves need peeling away carefully from the base of the trunk. Cabbage trees need good drainage: don't water them in winter or they will rot. 'Torbay Dazzler' has cream and grey stripes running down its leaves; 'Veitchii' crimson-flushed leaves; 'Purple Tower' broad plum-purple leaves.

Hosta

In recent years, hostas have come to mean 'slug-food', but growing them in pots is ideal; even if your garden is 'slug-city', running a thin copper strip discreetly round a pot will give off a little electrical charge and stop any slugs from climbing up! Grown primarily for their foliage, the many oval- to heart-shaped leaves grow in a symmetrical clump and range from green, blue-green, yellow, variegated to splashed and striped with cream and yellow. A good blue cultivar is 'Hadspen Blue'; *H. plantaginea* var. *japonica* (pictured) has lovely lime-green leaves. 'Sum and Substance' has yellow to yellow-green leaves, which pucker underneath when mature, and lilac flower spikes. Hostas prefer moist well-drained soil in full or partial shade. Plant them alone or in groups of containers for a bold effect.

***Imperata cylindrica* 'Rubra'**
If you're still wondering how to fit ornamental grasses into your borders, forget all about it and grow this one in a container – problem solved! This isn't just any old grass, either, but one that hails from tropical climes, so you'd be right to expect an exotic character. 'Rubra' spreads slowly, so won't need frenetic re-potting. It makes a clump of bright green leaves that measure 50cm (20in) long and about 3cm (1in) across. The tips turn blood-red, and then the rest of the leaves follow suit, colouring almost to the base until the whole plant is positively ablaze. Fluffy 20cm (8in) long panicles of silvery white flowers appear late in the summer to complete the look. Good moist soil rich in humus and a position in full sun/part-shade suit it well. A mulch will protect it in winter.

Lavandula angustifolia
Lavenders do well in containers in both formal and informal settings. Accommodating though the members of this species are, they're never boring, with their evergreen grey-green leaves, aromatic foliage and flowers that last for ages. They're also tolerant of neglect and won't scream if you forget to water them. You can clip them after flowering – don't cut into the old wood but just lightly clip the plant into a neat shape. Plant in good soil that's on the sandy side, and maybe slightly alkaline, and against a warm wall if you have a cold garden. *Lavandula angustifolia*, the most common species, has airy mauve flowerheads on long strong stems; 'Hidcote White' is more compact; 'Hidcote' (pictured) has dark purple flowers; 'Loddon Pink' soft pink flowers.

***Narcissus* 'Tête à Tête'**
There are many spring charmers among the narcissi and 'Tête à Tête' is one of the best. These bulbous perennials make a fabulous show of deep golden flowers. It's a small stocky vigorous daffodil about 15cm (6in) tall, often with two or three flowers, 7cm (2½in) across, per stem. Plant the bulbs in autumn at twice their depth. Bulbs in containers break all the rules of spacing, so you can cram them 3cm (1in) apart in a pot. Just remember to lift the bulbs once the leaves have died, and then replant them in August. This narcissus has no scent, but plenty do: 'Trevithian' and 'Quail' are both highly scented and very long-lasting. While other daffodils look good in the ground, this small one tends to get a bit lost, so growing it in a pot brings its beauty into close focus.

Pelargonium

Incorrectly known as geraniums, these are old cottage-garden favourites. Scented pelargoniums are especially lovely in pots placed along paths, where you can brush against the leaves to release their extraordinary scent. Some smell like oranges, lemons, even peppermint – and they are remarkably realistic. Old plants can become straggly, so pinch out the leaves when they're young to keep a good shape. 'Attar of Roses' is rose-scented (it really is!) and bears small mauve flowers in clusters. 'Lady Plymouth' (pictured) smells of lemons and has white-edged lime-green leaves. 'Pink Capitatum' has small lavender flowers and emits a sweet lime/rose fragrance when brushed against. Pelargoniums need protection from frost, but otherwise they're easy to look after.

Sasa veitchii

Not all bamboos are ideal for containers, but this one is. With its marauding rhizomes and eventual height and spread of 1.2m (4ft) in the garden, *S. veitchii* can be a thug on the run, but in a large robust container it is well behaved. Its broad lance-shaped leaves shoot from purple canes, and in autumn a curious thing happens: the leaves develop marked pale edges, making the plant appear variegated. This effect is due to the leaves withering away, but it's an attractive ageing process all the same! *Sasa* needs good moist well-drained soil, especially when grown in sun; it will also grow in deep shade. If you want *Sasa* in the garden border, grow it in a pot but bury it just below the surface of the garden soil – that'll stop you having a bamboo forest on your hands!

Tradescantia

Commonly grown as a trailing houseplant, this frost-tender evergreen perennial also has its uses outdoors. From June to the first frosts, *Tradescantia pallida* 'Purple Heart' will grow happily and rampantly in a window box or hanging basket. The purple stems grow jerkily downwards in a series of mini-elbow joints, sporting large 8–15cm (3–6in) oval leaves of a rich dark purple. In summer there are bright pink flowers; *T.* Andersoniana Group 'Osprey' (pictured) has large white flowers with a blue stamen. When it's growing well, pinch out the tips to encourage bushiness. All *Tradescantia*, especially the cultivars with coloured leaves, need lots of sun or the colour soon fades. Most need a good soil, lots of water and regular feeding to thrive.

ORNAMENTAL EDIBLES

So you don't have room for a vegetable patch in your city garden. So you think vegetables are the ugly sisters – especially in a garden where there are strong design elements. But you can have both, without tears. In your garden design it's possible to incorporate edible plants that are extremely decorative as well as being good to eat. And there's nothing more satisfying than picking something you've grown yourself and bringing it to the table. You just can't beat that fresh flavour! I'll be so bold as to say that all gardens can produce something good to eat.

The potager is the classic way to grow vegetables decoratively. Here, edibles are selected for their colour and form, and grown together in geometric arrangements, not in rows like conventional vegetable plots. Beds can be edged with clipped box (*Buxus*), chives, strawberries – anything you fancy!

Remember that a lot of flowers like marigolds and nasturtiums, as well as the blooms of pinks and pansies, can be eaten in salads, so why not incorporate these into your design? Some edibles are dramatic architectural plants, too: fennel, sweet corn, globe artichokes, squash, even courgettes.

If you have neither the room nor the inclination for dedicated vegetable growing, why not try herbs? These add such a fillip to the kitchen. Herbs look lovely grown together in raised beds, or in the sections of a cartwheel. They can be happily crammed into window boxes and pots, too. Sage, thyme and dwarf rosemaries all do well, and in summer you can grow basil and coriander leaf. Runner beans and peas grown up wigwams can take the place of more conventional flowering climbers, and act as decorative – as well as edible – focal points when repeated throughout the garden.

Always grow things you actually like to eat! It's surprising but many people grow vegetables they'd never normally buy from the shops. If you're short on space, then pick a few delicacies that taste just fabulous picked fresh and, with careful selection, you can find ones that have ornamental value, too.

All edible vegetables need good soil enriched with whatever you can dig in – compost, rotted manure, leafmould, and so on. And sun – don't forget that!

• To get a regular crop of your favourite salad, sow small amounts two to three weeks apart; that way you'll get a nice new crop as and when you want it, throughout the summer.

• If you have a greenhouse, a well-lit porch or vacant kitchen windowsill, you can start off some veggies in modules or small trays.

• Don't be tempted to grow the same crop in the same place year after year. Rotate their positions around the garden so that diseases don't build up.

• If you're interplanting salads and vegetables in ornamental borders, try to space them out or you'll end up with unsightly gaps everywhere once you've harvested them.

• Remember that all veggies grow much better and produce more crops if you give them lots of water. Once a week, add seaweed concentrate to your watering can for bumper yields and disease-resistant plants!

• Avoid using too many chemicals to control pests and diseases – remember that you're spraying something you're then going to eat! Just keep your plants healthy by watering them regularly, letting them have as much sun as possible, and clearing up dead leaves and debris to prevent nasty fungal diseases.

• The best way to get rid of a slug infestation is not to use chemicals, but to go slug-hunting. Arm yourself with rubber gloves, a torch and a bucket of salty water, and go out on summer nights. You'll pick up loads! As for slug pubs… what a waste! Drink the stuff yourself while you're on the prowl for the enemy.

PLANT PROFILES ORNAMENTAL EDIBLES

Apple (*Malus*)
For a south-facing wall, plant an apple tree if you want something that's edible as well as decorative. Grown in the open garden, your apple tree will look nothing special, but trained into a fan or other shape, you'll be maximising the visual appeal. For growing a fan against a wall, you'll need a dwarfing rootstock and very fertile soil. Fix horizontal wires to the wall 15cm (6in) apart, beginning at about 30cm (12in) above the soil. Buy a partially trained fan from a specialist nursery, and read about the necessary pruning work required to produce a stunning specimen! Don't be greedy for immediate crops as the pruning has to take precedence. 'Gala' is a medium-sized apple, bright orange with a red flush, juicy and with a rich flavour – delicious!.

Cherry (*Prunus cerasus* 'Morello')
It's nice to think that the bugbear of gardeners, the north wall, can be so productive and decorative. With the morello, the cooking cherry-pie variety of cherry, you have two for the price of one: training it in a fan or espalier against a wall is prettier and results in more fruit. It can also be grown in containers. Acid cherries fruit on one-year-old wood, so you'll need to remove a proportion of older wood each year. Buy your tree from a good nursery, telling them where you want to grow it and the available space. Some (expensive) trees will have been pruned to shape already; all you have to do is continue the process in spring and summer. Netting the fruit from birds is advisable. Most acid cherries are self-fertile, so you don't need another for pollination.

Chives (*Allium schoenoprasum*)
Thankfully, chives is easier to say than its Latin name! This is a popular herb, easy to grow and useful in garnishes and salads. It looks like a hollow-stemmed deep green grass growing in a graceful clump. Young leaves shoot very early in spring, reaching a height of 30cm (12in). In late spring/early summer, flower stalks send up tight little buds, which break open into balls of tufted purple-pink flowers, 3–5cm (1–2in) across. If you want more leaves than flowers, try to cut these off before they open; you'll probably lose the race in the end, though! Divide the plants in spring and they will bulk up nicely over summer. The foliage dies back after frost. *Allium tuberosum* (Chinese chives) has broader, flatter leaves and white round flower heads in August/September – a choice plant.

Fennel (*Foeniculum vulgare*)
Perennial fennel can reach huge proportions (1.5–2.2m/5–7ft), so site it carefully because it's tough to move when established. There's not much difference between the green variety and the bronze (*F. vulgare* 'Purpureum') – except the colour. Bronze fennel (pictured) works well as an architectural and dominant focal point in the mixed border. Fennel is pretty, from the new delicate spring growth right up to maturity. Tall, lush green stems are covered with fine feathery foliage, and late in summer yellow cow parsley-like flowers appear. The seeds are attractive and, even when they fall (it does self-seed), the plant skeleton still carries strong character and form. Fennel loves the sun and is fairly drought-tolerant. Grow *F. vulgare* var. *azoricum* for the classic fat bulbous vegetable.

Mint (*Mentha*)
All mints are invasive: that is, they spread to areas where they are not wanted – and fast! – which makes them ideal for containers. *Mentha* x *gracilis* 'Variegata', otherwise known as ginger, or red, mint isn't as vigorous as some, but you will still need to be mindful of where you plant it. It has red-tinted stems and tiger-like foliage flecked and striped with gold, which has a strong aroma and a pronounced ginger flavour. For culinary use, the soft round green leaves of applemint (*M. suaveolens*) are a good choice. Peppermint (*M.* x *piperita*) is tall and spreading with dark, almost black-tinged, stems. Fresh or dried, the leaves make a soothing digestive tea. Mint flowers in July/August, and gets smothered by obsessed bees and hoverflies. Mint tolerates poor soil, growing best in full sun, but part-shade will do.

Oregano (*Origanum*)
Herbaceous and summer-flowering, this perennial herb spreads to form neat mounds in sunny dry conditions. *Origanum vulgare*, also known as wild marjoram, has a somewhat woody spreading habit with small aromatic leaves and pink to white flowers borne in small clusters on branching stems. Bees, hoverflies and butterflies adore the flowers. 'Aureum' has pink flowers and bright pale gold leaves, and is not so vigorous, growing 30cm (12in) high. 'Aureum Crispum' is similar, but more spreading and with curly golden leaves. Sweet marjoram (*Origanum majorana*), pictured, has the best flavour for cooking but it doesn't tolerate heavy frosts. In late autumn, shear off the dead stems. Oregano flowers from June to August. Use it as groundcover at the front of a border.

Rosemary (*Rosmarinus officinalis*)
This woody evergreen, with short needle-like leaves and numerous small lilac-blue flowers, loves to be grown in a hot spot. On very warm days the essential oils in the leaves volatilise, and the resinous slightly spicy scent is set free around the bush. Large cultivars reach 2m (6ft), and their bark takes on an aged appearance. They lose their shape fast but, luckily, they are very amenable to pruning to shape. 'Miss Jessopp's Upright' is vigorous and one of the big cultivars; 'Prostratus' is low-growing, suitable for the top of a sunny wall or a sink garden. Rosemaries can survive frost, but if the soil is too wet, they may die. Topiary and hedging are possible, as is container-growing, even in window boxes for the lower-growing cultivars. They thrive against a south-facing wall.

Runner beans (*Phaseolus coccineus*)
In Victorian gardens these tender climbers, were grown for their pretty flowers, just like sweet peas, and the beans we eat today weren't allowed to develop. If you want a quick dense screen during summer, with the bonus of flowers and beans, this vigorous climber will do nicely. The flowers are scarlet, white, or bicoloured red and white. Choose stringless varieties like 'Desiree' or 'Polestar' for a better flavour. Germinate seed indoors in late spring, or sow outside, 15cm (6in) apart, after the last frost. Plants like rich soil, plenty of water and full sun. Their supports can be anything you like, as long as they're sturdy and fairly tall because runner beans live up to their name, reaching 3m (10ft). Rustic wigwams made from birch create vertical interest in cottage schemes.

Sage (*Salvia officinalis*)
Sages come from the Mediterranean and love to bake in the sun. If you have a dry stony parched patch of ground, try sage and other sun-loving herbs, like rosemaries and thymes. *Salvia officinalis* is the green culinary variety, with spikes of lilac-blue flowers in summer. However, all sages can be used in cooking. 'Purpurascens' (purple sage) has mulberry-red leaves that turn a dusty plum as the plant ages; 'Tricolor' (pictured), grey-green leaves with cream, pink and purple stripes; 'Icterina', variegated yellow-and-green leaves. All sages are aromatic and their leaves can be dried; the robust flavour is especially good for winter dishes. They do very well in window boxes and containers of all kinds, and you won't have to water them every five minutes! In the ground they will grow to 75cm (2½ft).

Strawberries (*Fragaria*)
All strawberries, especially the alpine varieties, make neat, functional and edible edging throughout the summer. Although short-lived, alpines are easy to grow from seed sown in spring. Sow them in pots and plant outside once they're big enough and the danger of frost has passed; they'll fruit the following year. The big fat juicy 'Wimbledon' strawbs like flavoursome 'Cambridge Favourite' (pictured) and disease-resistant 'Silver Jubilee' are best bought as potted rooted runners in late summer/autumn. You may get a few fruits the next year but expect big crops thereafter. Perpetual strawberries are ideal for containers. Alpines tolerate poor soil and semi-shade; all the others need lots of water to swell the fruit, and appreciate a humus-rich, fertile soil in the sunniest position.

Sweet corn (*Zea mays*)
Even though you usually see sweet corn in the vegetable patch, as it needs a lot of space, you can grow it as a tall architectural plant at the back of a border. Sweet corn has long leaves with white midribs and 'silks' of silver and bronzy hues. It can grow from 1.2–2.7m (4–9ft) tall. In a deep container filled with rich composty soil, you'll get a modest crop, and the plants are quite statuesque and attention-grabbing to look at without any cobs. Because they are wind-pollinated, sweet corn need to be grown in a group. They like full sun. 'Sugar Dots' has a reddish hue throughout the plant; 'Red Stalker' red and purple stalks; 'Striped Quadricolour' contrasting pink and white stripes on its leaves. 'Wampum' is a dwarf ornamental variety, with white husks and multicoloured tassels.

Tomatoes (*Lycopersicon*)
Particularly suitable for growing in pots, as long as they have the support they need, tomatoes are really worth growing, especially as our summers seem to be getting hotter. Nothing compares to the flavour of a sun-warmed tom popped straight in your mouth! Sow seed in early spring and keep frost-free. Plant out in May. You need to tie all tomato plants to strong supports, otherwise they flop and look untidy; bamboo tripods are ideal. Toms like good soil and a lot of water once the fruit has set, and the hottest place you can give them! Diseases can be a problem, so choose resistant varieties such as the small cherry tomatoes 'Gardener's Delight' and 'Cherry Belle'. 'Shirley' (pictured) is a big fat juicy tom, which is *very* disease-resistant and ideal for organic growers.

WATER • WATERSIDE

Some of the most dramatic plants are found either growing in water or on the edges of ponds. Among them are some enormous giants, straight out of the Jurassic period. Many are great for creating a jungle-style garden, provided you have the right growing conditions. The smaller ones are miniaturist treasures and can, like dwarf water lilies, be grown in tiny pools or barrels, or even old butler's sinks.

There's something about water-loving plants: they have such vigour and energy, even presence. If you have a pond, it doesn't look quite right unless the edge is lush with healthy foliage (unless the pond is a formal raised stretch of water). The bonus of having a pond are the insects, such as dragonflies, that water plants attract; other wildlife will gravitate to the pond margins, too.

If you have an area of garden that never dries out, don't drain it but turn it into a bog garden. Pile in the rotted manure and compost until you have a deeply cultivated soil – adding humus is a bit like adding a sponge to help retain the moisture so that it's always available for the bog plants.

You can create a bog garden next to a pond by digging out the area to a depth of at least 60cm (2ft) and to however wide you desire, and lining it with plastic in which you have made a few holes for drainage. Backfill with rich soil. The reason for keeping the bog area separate from the pond is that rich soil is not good for ponds and mustn't come into contact with the pond water – unless you like rich pea soup for water!

THE KNOW-HOW

Deep water plants (water lilies): Position these in baskets at the bottom of a pond but leave their leaves and flowers on the surface. They need a water depth of 30–100cm (1–3ft). Buy planting baskets at least 23cm (9in) in diameter for the roots to spread. They need repotting once every other year.

Marginals: Most marginals like 8–15cm (3–6in) of water over their crowns; deep marginals 30cm (12in) of water. Grow marginal plants, such as *Typha minima* and *Iris laevigata*, in the shallow water at the pond's edge.

Bog plants: Plants like *Lobelia cardinalis*, *Gunnera manicata* and *Ligularia* like moist soil and won't mind some serious waterlogging, although not for sustained periods. Grow them at the water's edge, so that their feet are wet and their tops dry, otherwise they'll rot. Many will grow happily in the herbaceous border, provided that it isn't too dry.

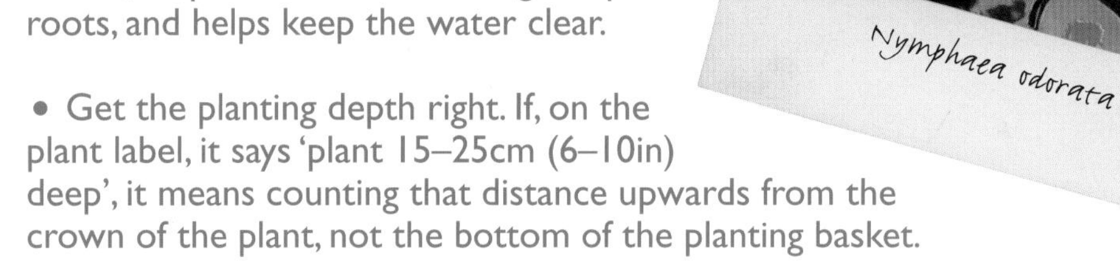

Nymphaea odorata

• Aquatic and marginal plants are best grown in special planting baskets. Use special aquatic compost, too. When you've finished planting, spread a layer of pea gravel all over the top of the soil. This helps keep the soil in the basket, stops fish from disturbing the plant roots, and helps keep the water clear.

• Get the planting depth right. If, on the plant label, it says 'plant 15–25cm (6–10in) deep', it means counting that distance upwards from the crown of the plant, not the bottom of the planting basket.

• Use bricks stacked on the bottom of the pond to give you the correct height for planting deep water aquatics and water lilies. Young specimens need planting more shallowly until they're established.

• Be especially careful when buying water lilies as the planting depth varies according to the size of the plant. Rule of thumb: leaves should float on the surface, not be submerged.

• Most plants that enjoy such wet conditions spread rapidly and can be invasive, so give them more room than you think they'll need.

• You'll probably have room for only one water lily, but you'll need to buy more marginal plants to provide bulk and lushness around the edges.

Acorus gramineus

The Japanese rush is a semi-evergreen aquatic perennial, with fans of shiny green, grass-like leaves 8–30cm (3–12in) long that produce a desirable lush effect at the water's edge. This is a foliage plant for the shallow margins of a bog garden, pool or sink garden. Use a planting basket and submerge it in water no more than 10cm (4in) deep. The rhizomes are used in Chinese medicine and European herbalism as an antibacterial and tonic herb, so this is a case for less showy plants having hidden depths! The cultivar 'Variegatus' (pictured) is striped cream and yellow; 'Ogon' makes a colourful waterside grass with cream-striped leaves; 'Pusillus' is a dwarf cultivar with stiff, compact green leaves. Contrast *Acorus gramineus* with the large leaves of hostas or *Ligularia*.

Filipendula purpurea

This is a garden variety of the common wild cream-flowered scented meadowsweet. It grows happily at the water's edge, reaching 1.5m (5ft), staying in a tidy clump. In July and August it bears carmine-red fluffy flowers, 5cm (2in) across, on tall crimson-purple stems above a clump of shapely five-pointed leaves. The flowers get paler as they age, but they stay a long time on the plant. *Filipendula* prefers a moist alkaline soil, but you can grow it in any soil, as long as you water in dry conditions. 'Purpurascens' has purple-tinted leaves; *F. purpurea* f. *albiflora* has white flowers. The stems and seeds can be left over winter, when they'll look good all frosted and cobwebby. An infusion of the dried leaves and flowers of the druid's favourite, *Filipendula ulmaria*, is great for an upset stomach!

Iris pseudacorus

The yellow flag is the original fleur-de-lys, emblem of the French kings and adopted by the Boy Scout movement. It's a deep, very vigorous marginal plant, growing on the edge of a pond or in wet places. The 1m (3ft) long leaves are ribbed and spear-shaped. Each branched stem bears 4–12 flowers, 8–10cm (3–4in) long. The petals are yellow, with brown or violet markings. 'Alba' has pale cream flowers; 'Variegata' white-and-yellow-striped leaves and brilliant yellow flowers; 'Bastardii' pale lemon flowers. After flowering, all plants produce ornamental brown seed capsules. Plant in good moist soil at the water's edge or in deeper water in sun or dappled shade. *Iris pseudacorus* looks good with hostas, the red-purple spires of *Lythrum salicaria* and a grass such as *Carex stricta* 'Bowles' Golden'.

Ligularia

From a large mound of round leaves with serrated edges, tall, almost-black, stems grow high above the foliage in early to late summer, to carry long cylindrical spires of small bright yellow flowers. Whether sited in damp soil in the herbaceous border or by the water's edge, this makes an imposing plant. A lot of waterside plants fall into the 'big' category, and this one does, too, so give it space to breathe! 'The Rocket' shoots up to 1.5m (5ft), and its yellow flowers with their lax petals have orange-yellow centres. 'Weihenstephan' has golden yellow flowers and is 30cm (12in) taller still; *L. przewalskii* (pictured) has small, yellow daisy-like flowers. Boggy conditions or just reliably moist soil suit *Ligularia* fine. It likes dappled shade, or full sun with midday shade. Shelter from strong winds.

Matteuccia struthiopteris

I call this 'Matt's-own dinosaur' plant, but its distinguished common names are the ostrich, or shuttlecock, fern. Suited to the pond edge or moist shade in neutral to acid soil, this deciduous fern sends up new fronds in spring from a thick tree trunk-like clump of vertical rhizomes. Each frond is finely divided and grows 1–1.5m (3–5ft) high. Shorter fronds of suede-brown appear in late summer and persist over winter, when the other leafy fronds die down. It spreads by rhizomes, and a mass of *Matteuccia* makes a primitive vertical frond forest, each frond a little sinister, uncurling at the tip like a green cobra rearing up to see what's happening. You want atmosphere? You got it! This is a fully hardy monster with good table manners.

Nymphaea

Water lilies are classic deep water plants with large open flowers, like many-petalled stars, blooming from June onwards. The crowns of large lilies need to be covered by 15–25cm (6–10in) of water, and those of small lilies by 8cm (3in) of water, so the leaves float on the surface. They like sunshine, a tranquil life and still water, otherwise they'll sulk and ail. Pick the right *Nymphaea* for the size of your pond: the leaves must have room to spread without overlapping, and some species are monsters! 'Virginalis' is a beautifully proportioned long-flowering white lily, suitable for a medium-sized garden pond; its flowers are fragrant with yellow stamens. 'Madame Wilfon Gonnère' (pictured) has pearly-pink flowers; 'James Brydon' clear crimson fragrant flowers.

Osmunda regalis

This is the biggest fern that can be grown outdoors in the UK: it produces 2m (6ft) high browny fronds, which are its flowers. The royal fern is a dominant, edge-of-the-water plant. On its own it contributes an architectural dimension; as part of a group of lush foliage plants, it brings a definite jungle look. The soil needs to be rich with compost, and kept that way. From the winter clump of black fibrous roots emerge fronds that uncoil as they grow, a buff-pink colour with creamy streaks of velvety down to begin with, turning green as they reach maturity. Fully hardy, the fern will survive in damp border soil that's slightly acid, but this mustn't dry out. 'Purpurascens' has red-purple flushed fronds in spring; 'Undulata' wavy segments.

Primula bulleyana

Primulas are a promiscuous lot in general, especially the candelabra primulas like *P. bulleyana*. If you grow several different species, you may find that an interesting range of colours crops up, all of mixed parentage. Along with irises and astilbes, *P. bulleyana* will add to the flower-colour range at the waterside from April to August. It has stout stems emerging from dark green leaves to produce whorls of 'art' shade flowers in orangey yellow, in June and July. You might sandwich the flowering in between *P. japonica* – the first candelabra primula to flower – and the later-flowering scented giant cowslip, *P. florindae*, for continuity of bloom. *Primula bulleyana* is a bog-loving herbaceous perennial needing reasonable, very moist/wet soil and a sunny position.

Rheum palmatum

Chinese rhubarb is an ornamental rhubarb that's not dissimilar to the edible kind, except it's bigger and more decorative. In spring great bosses of furled leaves unfold into large red-flushed frilly-fringed umbrellas 60–100cm (2–3ft)across. In June, a 2m (6ft) flowering stem bears a cluster of fluffy white flowers, followed by brown seeds. It's a water-holic, so plant it where its feet are not likely to dry out; it doesn't like flooding or constantly wet conditions, though! 'Bowles' Crimson' has dark red flowers, and leaves with a crimson underside. 'Atrosanguineum' has scarlet buds from which vivid crimson-purple young leaves emerge, followed by cerise-pink flowers. A big plant for jungle plantings or at the back of a large border, it can survive a northerly aspect and prefers sun/semi-shade.

Trillium

Everything about trilliums comes in threes: three leaves, three calyces (the cluster of modified leaves enclosing the flower bud) and three petals. Called wake-robin or toadshade, *T. sessile* forms clumps, with 12cm (5in) long stalkless leaves. Marbled pale green and milky white, or grey-white and a bronzy chocolate, the leaves alone are quite beautiful. Three leaves form a collar on which sit dark red-purple flowers. Seen from above, the whole resembles a small green plate with a sweet in the middle. Trilliums are striking, choice herbaceous perennials for a moist, shady border, liking neutral to acid soil. The flowers are borne in spring. *Trillium luteum* has yellow flowers; *T. ovatum* white. They need a cool shady place with a soil rich in leaf mould and always adequate moisture.

Typha minima

This is the baby bulrush, with all the character of its big brother *T. maxima*, except the robust size! A true marginal, it grows on the water's edge in mud, or water 30–45cm (12–18in) deep. Thick rhizomes spread in shallow water, and the fragile-looking but tough, very slender leaves, some 30–40cm (12–16in) long, emerge from them. The flowers are small, brown and furry, like little cocktail sausages on sticks, about 3cm (1in) long; its big brother's look more like the barbecue variety! *Typha minima* is the only species suitable for a small pond. You can also grow it in a tub or half-barrel, where its strong vertical lines provide a satisfying contrast to miniature water lilies. Use a planting basket and aquatic compost. The flowering stems can be dried for use in flower arrangements.

Zantedeschia aethiopica

The arum lily, which is so popular with brides, is a marginal aquatic suitable for ponds in mild areas. It needs a sunny position to thrive, and its roots must be kept frost-free; protect the fleshy crowns in winter with a thick layer of mulch. The glossy, deep green leaves are striking – they're heart-shaped and look just like the devil's tongue! The luminous white flowers, made up of a white spathe (a modified leaf) that surrounds a golden central spike, are produced from June onwards. 'Crowborough' (pictured) is hardier and more tolerant of dry conditions; 'Green Goddess' has large green flowers with white throats; 'Little Gem' is dwarf but produces tons more flowers. *Zantedeschia aethiopica* cultivars are graceful beauties, deserving pride of place in any pool.

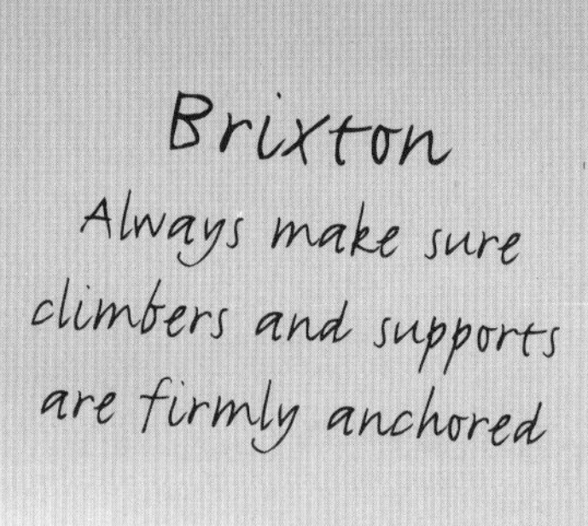
Brixton
Always make sure
climbers and supports
are firmly anchored

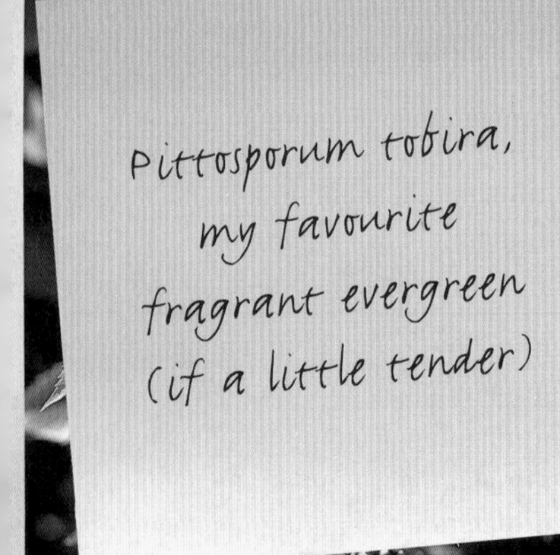
Pittosporum tobira,
my favourite
fragrant evergreen
(if a little tender)

No room for
vegetables and herbs?
Grow them in
containers!

BRIXTON

Sarah is an excellent cook and was longing to be able to entertain her friends outdoors. She wanted a garden with a Mediterranean 'outdoor room' feel.

As the budget was tight, I paved the eating area with imitation pre-cast concrete slabs in a terracotta colour instead of laying down expensive authentic tiles. Smaller blue-black tiles spaced uniformly break up the mass and lead the eye out into the garden.

The table and chairs are a dominant feature of the design. Sarah wanted a practical table, rather than a tiny decorative one, and although it rather swamps the garden, it does give Sarah more than enough room to entertain. While the space had to be seriously functional, it also had to look great from both the living room and the kitchen, so around the raised circle of paving I planted an eclectic mix of Mediterranean plants and those more usually grown in the UK. These included easy-to-grow herbaceous perennials, *Pittosporum tobira* and *Choisya ternata* 'Sundance'. Evergreen *Clematis armandii* and fragrant *Trachelospermum jasminoides* are trained up the walls and fences. I also included an ornamental crab apple – something that Sarah was very keen on. To create a sense of balance and complete the look, I filled terracotta containers with culinary herbs, and steel 'air balloons' smothered in ivy.

PUTTING YOUR PLANTS TOGETHER

Gardening is all about getting stuck in, being 'dirty-hands creative', as I call it. And this is never more so than when you plan and implement your own planting schemes. For many people, myself included, plants are the most pleasing part of a design. Hard landscaping is the 'foundation', whereas the plants are the 'decorations' – a chance to really experiment with shape, colour and texture. The previous chapter showed you a smidgen of the plant world; some of the plants are traditional favourites, others you may have never seen or heard of before. But the big question now is: How do you put your chosen plants into a planting scheme that works?

This chapter looks at the key points to consider when planning a planting scheme, but I want to emphasise that making a border is not an exact science; it's more about expressing your own taste in a coherent way. Borders are often created piecemeal or as an on-going and ever-changing process – it really doesn't matter. So don't expect to find the definitive answers to all your questions here; the chapter is intended merely to help you organise your planting a little more consciously.

LOOK AROUND YOU

The best way to start is by looking at the successes of others. Gardening books will help, as will trips to the many private gardens around the country open to the public. But you can also look closer to home. Look at how your neighbours arrange **colours and leaf shapes**, where they use focal points and architectural plants. Make a note, too, of those planting combinations that don't work.

Making a plan, even a simple sketch, is invaluable. This will help you decide where to position your plants, how they'll relate to each other size-wise, and how many you might need to buy. You don't want to cram plants in; you'll end up with a maintenance problem. Nor do you want to underplant, leaving unsightly gaps, which might take years to fill out. You need to find a happy medium.

Devote lots of **time and thought** to choosing your plants. If you make loads of impulse buys, chances are you'll end up with lots of costly mistakes or wince every time you look out on the chaos you've created. The temptation to start planting can be overwhelming, but wait until you've finished the hard landscaping. New plantings will only get in the way and, more often than not, get trashed.

Although you may have already decided which plants you'd like, do check that they're suitable for your space before you buy them. Select only those plants that suit the characteristics of your garden. (The plant lists in the next chapter will help you make the right choices according to your soil, garden orientation and aspect.) Most plants are, however, fairly tolerant: a plant that likes full sun will also tolerate some shade for part of the day. And plants are very amenable to being moved about to better homes if they haven't been doing too well.

• Pick plants that are suited to your location: shade-lovers for shady spots, sun-lovers for sunny places, bog plants for really damp areas. *Escallonia* and *Olearia* are ideal for windswept seaside locations, whereas hybrid tea roses will hate it. Planting a sun-loving *Canna* in a cold bog-garden won't work, in the same way that planting a choice grapevine on a north-facing wall is asking for trouble.

• Choose plants suitable for your soil: *Rhododendron* and *Azalea* for acid soils, roses for rich clay soils, *Clematis* and *Buddleia* for alkaline soils. It's pointless planting something that prefers a different soil type – it'll only struggle to survive.

• Are the plants suitable for the function you have in mind? Will that climber neatly cover the fence, or will it romp away and quickly smother the garage as well? And the perfumed plant you bought for the alfresco dining area: is it sweetly scented, or do you privately think it stinks?

• Will the plants you like cause problems with foundations or drains, etc? Don't plant willows, limes or *Eucalyptus* close to buildings.

• Have you enough space to accommodate a plant when it grows to maturity? Don't grow huge monsters like *Gunnera* if they'll soon swamp the garden. You can grow some unruly customers like *Forsythia* and *Buddleia davidii* because they will tolerate a hard prune, but if they are allowed to grow unchecked, they, too, will soon take over the garden.

• Don't be tempted to fill the garden to overflowing right from the start. If you do, you'll end up with a garden where only the fittest survive and all the delicate plants will end up swamped in the ensuing fight for nutrients, light and elbowroom.

• Do the plants that you're considering suit your ideas of garden maintenance? For example, is this a plant that needs loads of TLC, or will it thrive despite you being away for weeks at a time?

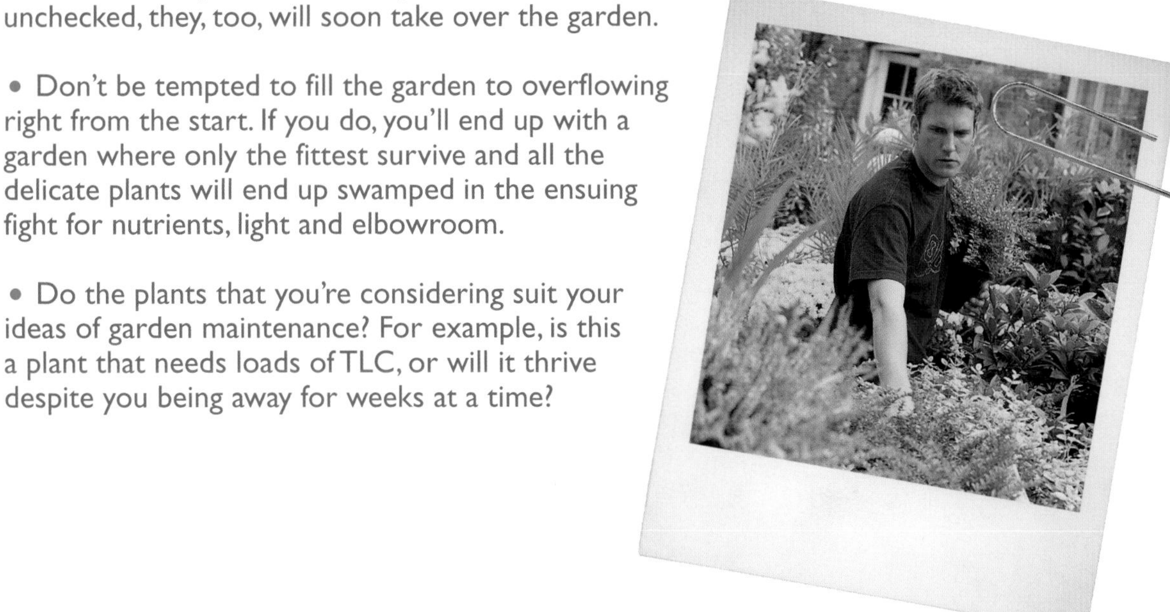

THE MIXED GARDEN

In the small city garden, year-round interest is important, especially where everything is on view. Try to create something that will **surprise and delight** right through the year, even in winter. But although it's great to have interest in the garden all year round, there are occasions when there is nothing more impressive than huge bursts of seasonal colour. Spring wouldn't be the same if it weren't for the massed ranks of trumpet daffodils, and summer just begs to have spectacular herbaceous border plantings.

Although you may not go into the garden a great deal, it is still a picture to be viewed from the house. Depending on the design, the planting can be incredibly diverse, using trees, shrubs, roses, grasses, perennials and bulbs to **sparkle at different times**.

FLOWERS

You might choose lots of bulbs like snowdrops, crocuses, wood anemones (*Anemone blanda*) and small narcissi like 'February Gold' or 'Tête à Tête' for spring. Following these in early summer you could have bearded iris, *Geranium* 'Johnson's Blue' and an architectural plant like bear's breeches (*Acanthus mollis*), with bergamot (*Monarda*), yarrow (*Achillea*) and blue globe thistle (*Echinops ritro*) for late summer. For autumn, there could be shrubs like *Fatsia*, *Fuchsia* and *Carpenteria californica*, followed by *Chimonanthus praecox*, *Lonicera fragrantissima* and *Viburnum* x *bodnantense* 'Dawn' – three deciduous beauties whose flowers fill the air with a deliciously sweet scent throughout winter.

Continuity of flowering is a difficult act to manage when you're first starting out; you need to study plant profiles to work out what flowers when, and for how long, and then note how they all dovetail. The secret is to choose some plants with a **long flowering season** so, if you don't get it spot-on, it doesn't matter. Japanese anemones and *Verbena bonariensis* are perfect, as are repeat-flowering roses like 'Iceberg' (white) and 'Queen Elizabeth' (pink), and climbers like *Clematis montana* 'Grandiflora' (white) or *Clematis tangutica* 'Bill MacKenzie' (yellow) whose seed heads also look stunning. Regular visits to your local nursery will help; you'll be able to see what's flowering and at what time – just leave the chequebook at home!

Hypericum x inodorum 'Rheingold'

FOLIAGE & BERRIES

Flowers are not the only source of interest, however; the well-designed mixed garden uses everything a plant has to offer. In autumn, shrubs like *Euonymus alatus* and witch hazels are a must as their dull green foliage turns to **flamboyant reds, oranges and golden yellows.** For a real autumnal wow!, nothing beats a Japanese maple. Planted in the centre of a border the brilliant colours of the dying leaves will light up the ground. Plants with attractive berries are a must for this time of year, too: *Cotoneaster*, hollies and *Pyracantha* all catch the eye with bright red, orange or yellow berries, which last right through to early spring. For berries like no other, choose *Callicarpa bodinieri* var. *giraldii* – an unassuming deciduous shrub for most of the year but, come winter, it's covered in metallic purple fruit – a real horticultural freak!

STEMS & BRANCHES

The colour of stems and branches also becomes important in the mixed garden, especially in winter. Snake bark maples like *Acer davidii* 'Serpentine' (with dark purple shoots in spring), or 'Ernest Wilson' have white-streaked bark in deepest winter. *Prunus serrula* has stunning ruby-red bark, which seems almost luminous in the low winter sun. Other plants noted for their bark include *Rubus cockburnianus*, the white-stemmed ornamental bramble, and dogwoods like *Cornus alba* 'Elegantissima' (variegated leaves, red stems) and *Cornus stolonifera* 'Flaviramea' (yellow stems), which have an amazing stem colour if they're cut back hard in spring.

Drifts of variegated sage, orange daylilies and silver cotton lavender surrounding a flowering dogwood

FRAMEWORK PLANTS

Like the garden as a whole, mixed planting schemes need a structural backbone to hold them together. Invariably this is made up of strategically positioned evergreens, hedges or small trees. Think of these as the framework plants in a border; they might not give you drama or flashy flowers, but they do give **vital support** for everything else. And most of these backbone plants will need little maintenance… as long as you take their eventual size into account when planting. Omitting the structural backbone from your planting is the equivalent of omitting the sand and cement when laying a patio: a pile of slabs chucked in a heap doesn't make a good seating area!

TREES & SHRUBS

At the back of the border you could plant *Olearia* x *haastii* (daisy bush), *Viburnum* x *burkwoodii* 'Anne Russell', acid-loving *Camellia* 'Shiro-wabisuke' or *Choisya arizonica* 'Goldfinger', all of which are well-behaved, mound-forming evergreen shrubs growing to no more than 3m (10ft) in height. Choose yew (*Taxus baccata*), holly (*Ilex aquifolium* 'J. C. van Tol' is a particularly good one), Portuguese laurel (*Prunus lusitanica*) or *Camellia japonica* 'Adolphe Audusson' for something taller. If left unchecked, all these plants can grow to 7m (23ft) or more. If that sounds a bit too monstrous, simply clip them into a hedge to **control their size**.

Structural plants shouldn't just be resigned just to the fence line, though. Clipped box cones or columnar yew (*Taxus baccata* 'Standishii') can provide a **three-dimensional frame** when placed near the front of a border. In this position, they will lightly conceal part of the planting behind, introducing a sense of mystery.

Use evergreens sparingly as too many will overwhelm smaller perennials and annuals. How many you use depends upon the style of garden you're after. In oriental gardens, you'll be hard pushed to find something that isn't an evergreen. In cottage gardens, they are used far more cautiously; they blend seamlessly into the background, letting flowering shrubs and herbaceous perennials like foxgloves, lupins and delphiniums take centre stage.

BRIGHTEN 'EM UP

With careful choice of climbers, you can easily enliven even the dullest evergreen throughout the summer: try growing *Lapageria rosea* (Chilean bellflower) through a firethorn or holly, or climbing nasturtiums through dark conifers (*Tropaeolum speciosum* likes the shady side of such trees, whereas *T. peregrinum* likes the sunny side).

PLANTING IN TIERS

Most borders are traditionally planted in tiers or layers, with taller plants at the back, so they don't conceal smaller ones at the front. Planting in tiers adds a **sense of movement** to a border. You start at the front, and then subtle changes in height lead the eye up into the canopy of trees behind, each plant acting as a foil for the ones in front. It's the most logical way of combining plants of different heights. Just remember the school photo: beefy chaps at the back, small guys at the front. In narrow spaces, a mass of plants all the same height only emphasises the lack of space, and just appears static.

WHAT GOES WHERE?

Typically, small trees, tall grasses and larger evergreens make up the back layer; smaller deciduous shrubs and larger herbaceous perennials like *Achillea*, *Artemisia ludoviciana* (white sage) and *Filipendula* (meadowsweet) the middle; and low-growing plants like dead nettle (*Lamium*), *Primula*, *Tiarella* and hostas carpeting the front and helping to keep weeds down. Evergreen wall shrubs and climbers, like *Garrya elliptica* 'Evie', *Clematis cirrhosa* var. *balearica* and ivy are commonly grown against walls and fences.

To achieve a **natural gradation** that pulls the eye into the border, try out some combinations at your local garden centre. Don't feel that by moving loads of plants around, you're being naughty. Most garden centres are very accommodating, plus it's your money, so just make sure you're happy. Check out the height of your chosen plants when fully grown, then plan accordingly, keeping in mind how each one relates to its neighbours when it comes to colour, shape and form. In island beds, the principle is still the same, with taller structural plants positioned in the centre, and the other plants following in circular tiers that splay out down to groundcover at the front.

SHADY BORDER

A simple tiered border for a shady bed backed by a north-facing wall might have *Hydrangea petiolaris* (self-supporting climber, with **deciduous glossy leaves** and panicles of off-white flowers in early summer) growing against the wall. In front, Japanese anemones like *Anemone* x *hybrida* 'Honorine Jobert' or *Anemone hupehensis* var. *japonica*. The next tier could be made up of yellow-flowered day lilies (*Hemerocallis* 'Corky', 'Golden Chimes', 'Bitsy'; most day lilies like full sun but these cultivars tolerate shade) planted around a squat evergreen like *Prunus laurocerasus* 'Otto Luyken'. Near to the front, large drifts of the snowflake *Leucojum aestivum* (spring bulbs like tall snowdrops), interplanted with *Geranium clarkei* 'Kashmir White' (shade-tolerant geranium flowering in late spring to midsummer) and *Pulmonaria* 'Mawson's Blue' (dense clusters of violet-blue flowers). Right at the

A classic tiered border, including sage, thyme, pinks, asters, *Verbena bonariensis*, mallow and a red floribunda rose

front, overflowing onto a gravel path, could be *Pachysandra terminalis* (Japanese spurge), *Helleborus orientalis* (Christmas rose) for winter interest and numerous rivers of purple *Ajuga*. This mix of plants will provide interest right throughout the year.

SUNNY BORDER

For a sunnier spot, the backbone could be a couple of *Pittosporum* 'Garnetii' flanked by tall *Miscanthus sacchariflorus*; in front, *Knautia macedonica* 'Melton Pastels', an unruly herbaceous perennial ideal for the back of a border, especially when you allow it to sprawl through structural evergreens. The middle tier could be a **sea of French lavender** (*Lavandula stoechas*) surrounding any number of box cones and evergreens like *Viburnum davidii* (dense, blue-black berries in winter) and *Pittosporum tobira* 'Nanum'. The front could be a mixture of *Lamium maculatum* 'Roseum' (white-variegated leaves with rose flowers) and *Heuchera* 'Chocolate Ruffles'. For a contrast in texture, plant a small golden grass like *Stipa tenuissima* (30–40cm/12–16in tall) in graceful clumps throughout. For further seasonal interest, plant white *Lilium regale* for summer in the middle layer and small white snowdrops for spring down at the front in among the deep purple foliage of the *Heuchera*. The possibilities are endless!

Informal drifts of foxgloves, cranesbill, *Euphorbia*, coneflowers and mixed grasses

SHOW RESTRAINT WITH YOUR CHOICE OF PLANTS

DRIFT & PRAIRIE PLANTING

Many annuals and perennials are best planted in drifts to appreciate them fully. Some don't hold up well as individual specimens; on their own they can look straggly, insignificant, even weedy. But planted en masse they make a **bold statement** and balance out taller and denser plantings of evergreens and conifers.

Don't plant too many different varieties together. Drifts of annuals and perennials are appreciated for their size, and too many different types in a small garden will make it appear cluttered and unplanned. Large drifts are ideal for contemporary and minimalist designs that rely on bold simple expanses of planting.

Prairie planting has taken the concept of drift planting to its extreme. Based on the open prairies of the American Midwest, or traditional wildflower meadows, prairie planting combines ornamental grasses with tough herbaceous perennials like golden rod (*Solidago*), yarrow (*Achillea*) and *Rudbeckia*. Planted in large swathes and usually bursting with colour, drift planting is the way of the naturalistic gardener. On a smaller scale choose **slender transparent beauties** like *Thalictrum* (meadow rue), *Cimicifuga simplex* 'Scimitar', *Persicaria polymorpha* or *Gaura lindheimeri*, which are like clouds of mist, and don't obscure the plants behind. While prairie planting is breathtaking, achieving continuity of display right through the year can be difficult unless you use lots of evergreen grasses, like *Deschampsia cespitosa* 'Goldtau' (hairgrass), *Stipa arundinacea* (pheasant's tail grass) and *Miscanthus floridulus*, or plants like *Agapanthus*, *Eupatorium purpureum* 'Atropurpureum' and *Veratrum nigrum*, which look good in winter.

Candelabra primulas en masse

SHAPE & FORM

When you plant in tiers, it's all too easy to succumb to rigid uniformity, resulting in your border looking like a staircase. So the shape of your plants is important; it will have a dramatic effect upon the composition of your planting scheme, and help to break it up and make it more three-dimensional. Strategic placing of architectural plants will **bring your border to life**; a pencil juniper, with its striking vertilinear thinness, will make a great focal point, at the same time drawing your attention to the carpet of flowers around it. Or why not use two, as sentries, either side of a path?

Other plants like spiky *Phormium*, *Cordyline* and the Spanish dagger (*Yucca gloriosa* 'Variegata') add a sense of drama and contrast when planted in among rounded shapes. Grasses, bamboos and erect perennials like *Ligularia* 'The Rocket' (yellow flowers) and *Kniphofia* (red-hot poker) do the same. Or you can use cane wigwams, with sweet peas scrambling up them, to give height where needed. Strategically placed pots of bamboo or tall grasses can be moved to wherever you want them. *Clematis* can be grown up freestanding pyramids of trellis, or *Wisteria* can be grown as a standard.

By using lots of different plants of the same habit, you can create a carpet effect gently stretching out over a large area. This can mesmerise when done well. Broken up by the occasional placement of tall *Verbascum olympicum*, *Crambe cordifolia* or *Veronicastrum*, it's similar to prairie planting, but more reminiscent of the South African veldt swathed in its brilliantly coloured flowers.

Architectural interest doesn't just come from the form of the plant as a whole; also important is the **shape of the leaves**. *Fatsia japonica* has huge hand-shaped leaves, while those of *Gunnera* are ribbed and umbrella-like – large enough to shelter under! And you wouldn't want to get too close to the spiky leaves of *Yucca gloriosa*!

Some plants can be clipped to provide architectural interest: box, azaleas, yew, shrubby honeysuckle (*Lonicera pileata*) can all be trimmed into whatever shape you want. Fruit trees can be espaliered, and some trees can even have their upper branches pruned into cube shapes... planted in parallel lines, these make highly attractive walkways.

Many gardeners see form as being more important than flower; like an evergreen, form is 'always there', whereas flowers come and go. But the art is to **use architectural plants sparingly**, so they'll jump out of the planting and catch the eye. Too many, and a border will look restless. Soften them with dainty grasses and herbaceous perennials, if you need to.

TYPICAL CENTRE-STAGE PLANTS

Aesculus parviflora • *Aralia elata* • bamboos • *Corylus avellana* 'Contorta' • *Euphorbia characias* • *Euphorbia mellifera* • *Fatsia japonica* • *Gunnera manicata* • *Magnolia delavayi* • *Phormium* • *Photinia* x *fraseri* 'Red Robin' • *Stipa gigantea* • *Viburnum plicatum* 'Mariesii' • *Yucca filamentosa*

Variegated *Nasturtium* and spiky *Yucca*

FRAGRANCE

Unless a plant has such a free fragrance that it drifts all over the garden, don't plant **scented gems** at the back of a border; you won't be able to get to them easily for a good sniff! Position them close to where you walk and sit. That way you will catch the scent without even trying too hard. Good places are by the front door, by the side of a path, next to a bench, around an outdoor dining area and at the front of borders. For a guaranteed delicious whiff, grow powerfully free-scented plants like *Lilium regale*, *Sarcococca humilis* and *Mirabilis jalapa* in containers, so you can move them to wherever the action is.

Use plants that release their scent at those times when you're most often in the garden. For anyone out at work all day, plants that release their real wallop of scent in the evening are ideal. Choose those that are **generous with their fragrance** so you unconsciously get a whiff without realising. It'll then lead you on a quest to find the fragrant offender!

For a lemony smell, grow long-lasting evening primrose (*Oenothera biennis*). The strong sweet scent of moonflower (*Ipomoea alba*) is unmistakeable, and is a must for the true night garden; the large white flowers slowly open at sunset and retreat as morning breaks. But, for me, the best of all evening fragrances has to be that of the night-scented stock (*Matthiola bicornis*): the flowers are really nothing much to look at during the day, but in the evening they release a fabulous coconut-ice scent that will perfume the entire garden.

Lilium henryi and yellow daylilies

Statice, *Ageratum* and cornflowers in the front of a harmonious planting scheme

Make good use of vertical space, and smother walls and fences in free-scented climbers. On sunny walls, grow *Jasminum* x *stephanense*; on shady walls, *Lonicera japonica* 'Halliana'. But do check before you buy; not all jasmines and honeysuckles are sweetly perfumed; some have no scent at all.

USING COLOUR

Colour is perhaps the trickiest aspect of designing a successful planting scheme – there are just so many plants in so many different colours! Being spoilt for choice can lead to confusion, begging the perennial question of 'Does this colour "work" with that one?' I often get in a muddle when putting a colour scheme together, and I guarantee you'll feel the same! But you needn't worry. Nature's own harmoniser, the colour green, is at hand. Green has to be the **most adaptable colour** on the planet. It's the perfect backdrop colour, which means that we often take it for granted, but using lots of green in a garden is a clever way to ensure we don't have those colour clashes sometimes found in our wardrobes! Green has the extraordinary ability to smooth, harmonise, and sort out the differences between warring factions. And it also has an extremely large palette all of its own: from light gold-greens, through glaucous-blue greens, to dense greens that appear almost black.

Stipa gigantea and *Verbena bonariensis*

Coreopsis grandiflora 'Early Sunrise' and heliotrope

Orange *Helenium* and *Achillea filipendula*

Sea holly and *Allium cristophii*

THE COLOUR WHEEL

Colour is, of course, a matter of personal preference, but for beginners and more experienced gardeners alike the colour wheel can help immensely in the decision-making process. It's ideal if you want to create colour effects in a more conscious way, and not just rely on 'happy accidents'. Look on it as a 'comfort blanket', something you can count on and refer to if you think your judgement is a little askew. Remember, flowers aren't the only source of colour. Leaf colour, bark, berries and seed heads, all contribute to the picture.

Complementary colour schemes use colours that are directly opposite each other on the wheel. Think of the golden hop (*Humulus lupulus* 'Aureus') growing into the canopy of the purple filbert *Corylus maxima* 'Purpurea', or blue *Agapanthus* interplanted with orange lilies (*Lilium henryi*) among *Nepeta* 'Six Hills Giant'. Complementary groupings are always dramatic and stimulating, especially if the colour is seasonal. Opposites often bring out the best in each other!

Monochromatic colour schemes use different shades, tints and hues of only one colour. You might use white *Eryngium giganteum*, the scented regal lily (*Lilium regale*), *Convolvulus cneorum*, *Salvia coccinea* 'White Lady', and tough but unruly *Cerastium tomentosum*, for example. But although monochromatic schemes are 'safe' and create a crisp, sophisticated look, restricting yourself to one colour makes it tough when you take into account the soil, aspect, and orientation of your garden.

Polychromatic planting schemes throw caution to the wind and include lots of different colours from all around the wheel: big splashes of red, blue, orange and yellow all mixed together, using the colour green to link them. Here's the chance to have fun and experiment with combinations that either complement, contrast, or clash with each other. It's a colour riot!

Harmonious or analogous planting schemes consist of colours that are adjacent to each other on the colour wheel, such as orange, yellow and red, or pink, violet, and blue. As each colour shares similar pigments, it's the easiest way to create a planting scheme that works. The effect is usually peaceful and gentle, so schemes using related colours are ideal in those areas of the garden where you want to relax. These are similar bedfellows living in harmony.

THE EFFECT OF COLOUR

Colour has a profound effect on our mood. We know this from the clothes we select from day to day. Warm colours like red and orange are exciting, and make us feel bright-eyed and bushy-tailed. A massed planting of warm colours seen from a distance is **breathtaking**. This is hot stuff, although their success does depend upon where you use them. In sunny spots they jump out, socking you between the eyes, but in deep shade they can disappear, especially tones of violet and red.

Blue, green, soft pink and lilac are cool colours. They blend into the background, and help to add distance, which makes a small space feel larger. For a calming effect, try mixtures of soothing blues like *Brunnera macrophylla, Echinops ritro, Polemonium caeruleum* (Jacob's ladder), and *Geranium* 'Johnson's Blue'.

I love combining feminine pinks and purples: globe-shaped *Allium hollandicum* 'Purple Sensation' and *Digitalis purpurea* rising up through a sea of *Knautia macedonica* 'Melton Pastels' and underplanted with self-heal (*Prunella* 'Pagoda') and purple sage (*Salvia officinalis* 'Purpurascens), for example, are just perfect for an early summer colour scheme. If you haven't already guessed, *Verbena bonariensis* is one of my favourite plants; it has a wonderful **tall and stately shape**, a long flowering season and sprays of iridescent purple flowers that look magical when falling through a tall oatmeal-coloured grass like *Stipa gigantea*, which lends it the support it needs.

Silver and white, like green, are wonderful colours for easing the tension between shouting oranges and yellows. Alone, they can appear a little stark, but grouped with warm and cool colours, they become another of nature's great harmonisers.

Dark colours make a garden feel shorter, whereas white at the bottom of the garden makes it feel longer. If your garden is used only at night, choose colours like white and yellow that don't fade as it gets dark; blues are the first colours to disappear as the sun goes down .

ORNAMENTS

Sculpture in the garden needs to be chosen with more care than the ornaments you select for your house. Most probably you will have far fewer ornaments in the garden, so they will stand out more. And sculptures, whether abstract or not, will attract more attention among the plants than you might expect. So what looks good? Bold forms in **natural materials**, whether willow sculptures or terracotta urns, blend in nicely. Colours like deep pink or cobalt blue will draw the eye and give contrast to the preponderance of green. You could class a container full of plants as an ornament, but containers left empty look fine, too, as long as the container is architectural in its own right. But these are safe ornaments. What about something a little more avant-garde? Well, try out your fancy, and see where it fits – you'll find out by trial and error.

DON'T LEAVE THEM 'TIL LAST

The furnishings for the garden are often an afterthought. After all, they don't appear as important as the skeleton planting. But they should be considered from the outset since they help define the style of your garden. And if you have a particular sculpture or ornament you want in the garden, that ornament might well determine what style of garden you go for.

If the garden is modern, you can take risks with focal-point abstract sculptures, and design features in glass, stainless steel, copper. If the garden is more cottagey, go for natural materials.

- Large terracotta urns go particularly well in formal gardens; they also make strong focal points.

- Glazed ceramic pots work well with oriental-style gardens, and enliven large expanses of brick or driveways.

- Half-barrels are excellent containers for cottage gardens and, surprisingly, can work well in oriental-style settings (especially if used as a small pond with a few goldfish, or planted with bamboo).

- Statues, and other objets d'art, act as strong focal points. Wooden statuary, either abstract or formal, goes well with country-style settings; fired clay and marble fit formal gardens; metal complements minimalist and modern designs.

- Water features go with every design. A water feature can be as formal as you like (ornate classical mask acting as a water spout, straight narrow rills à la Alhambra, rectangular raised ponds à la Versailles); or as informal (natural-looking wild-life pond, cascading stream bounded by lush waterside planting). For ultra-modern designs, create a raised rectangular pond with reflective metal edging, or have large glass spheres with water from a hidden pump pulsing over the top.

LIGHTING

An inner city garden bounded by walls can so easily work as an outdoor room – one that can be used and enjoyed even after the sun has gone down. So why not add another dimension to your planting by incorporating some **clever exterior lighting**? Choose from inexpensive low-voltage plastic sets, which you can wire up yourself, to costly ones crafted in brushed steel and copper that require a qualified electrician to install them. Solar-powered lights are an inexpensive alternative, but they can be a little temperamental. The main point in their favour, though, is that you don't need to fork out for an electrician.

UPLIGHTING

Uplighting trees is a great idea, especially those with interesting bark like *Prunus maackii* (Manchurian bird cherry) and *Prunus serrula* (Tibetan cherry), or those with light translucent foliage like the cut-leaf silver birch (*Betula pendula* 'Laciniata') or the wedding cake tree (*Cornus controversa* 'Variegata'). Position a spotlight at the base of the trunk so that it lights up the bark. Why have a focal point that you really only notice during the day?

IN THE SPOTLIGHT

Use blank white walls as a projector screen, and focus spotlights on architectural gems like *Eriobotrya japonica* (loquat) or grasses with long leaves like *Miscanthus* 'Morning Light' and the straw-coloured *Molina caerulea* 'Heidebraut' – the show starts when the leaves are tickled by the wind. For a ghostly effect, direct spotlights through low planting. In secluded corners, this will give your garden an almost unearthly feel.

Water and lighting go hand in hand. Place waterproof spotlights in still pools for a supernatural glow, or under fountains or spouts to produce a **shimmering effect**. If your pond is large enough, position lights so the water mirrors focal points, like simple urns or statues. Many waterproof lights have different-coloured filters, so why not go for a multicoloured effect?

DO-IT-YOURSELF LIGHTS

For those on a really tight budget, grab anything to hand and get creative. Train exterior fairy lights up into trees or over arches and pergolas, to define their shape. For simple garden flares, push church candles into lengths of copper tubing, or puncture old tin cans and pop a tea light in them. Position them around the garden in **informal groups**. These are just a few suggestions; the possibilities of do-it-yourself lights are endless.

GETTING A RHYTHM TO THE PLANTING

This can be achieved by repeating certain plants: clipped box balls at the corners of rectangular beds, a row of lavenders at the front of a meandering bed, clumps of purple-leaved sage planted throughout a border. Or you can use colour schemes to flow through the planting in patterns, with groupings of blue flowers merging into groupings of pink-flowering plants. Or **juxtapose shapes** and form, mounding azaleas next to erect bamboo. Alternate heights: fastigiate purple *Berberis* next to floppy mounds of blue-flowering catmint, repeated throughout. It's up to you to experiment, and see what you like best. Resist the temptation to buy every plant that catches your eye – self-discipline is essential – and don't plump for too many colours or different shapes, otherwise your planting scheme will appear chaotic and therefore uncomfortable to look at.

PREPARATION FOR PLANTING

Once you have planned your scheme, you can get planting but, first, you'll need to look at your soil, the lifeblood of any garden (see also pages 20–1). Contrary to popular belief, there is no such thing as a 'bad' soil. It's true, some soils are difficult to manage, but look at the plant world as your ally. I guarantee that even if you have thick clay, there are plants that'll romp away, so don't despair. Your soil will become a problem only if you choose plants that don't actually like it.

The best time to prepare a border for planting is **late autumn**, to give the soil a chance to settle and the weather to break down large clods of earth, ready for spring planting. If you can't wait that long, it really doesn't matter, but don't work the soil when it's waterlogged, as you'll damage its structure.

• Clear the area where you want to begin work. Get rid of oil spills, glass, lumps of concrete and old rotten timber. And don't forget to dig up any orange building sand that may have been left behind – it's full of nasties that all plants hate.

• Dig up any existing shrubs and perennials and put to one side; you might want to use them later. Try to take them out with as much soil as possible and cover them temporarily with soil or straw, to prevent the roots from drying out.

• Map out the shapes of your flowerbeds and borders. Regular geometric shapes are static; they hold the eye and are ideal for formal gardens. Irregular or freeform shapes give a feeling of movement. Remember to keep scale and proportion in relation to the size of your border and the garden as a whole.

• Make sure you're rid of perennial weeds like couch grass and ground elder; dig out every last bit with a gardening fork, or spot-weed with a translocated weedkiller containing glyphosate. Remove any turf and, if you don't want to reuse it, stack it out of the way where it will rot down into good compost.

• Dig in as much organic matter as you can. This might be well-rotted horse manure, leaf mould, spent hops, mushroom compost – whatever you can lay your hands on. It's hard work and often a bit smelly, but it'll help your plants no end. You can rake in any topsoil you saved when you dug out patios and ponds.

• Once you've dug the plot over, ideally to the depth of a spade, rake it out with the back of a fork and break up any remaining clods. Then use a rake to make the surface nice and crumbly. Contour your beds if you need to. Then stamp all over it! Using your heels, shuffle across this nicely raked soil to consolidate it. This removes any air pockets, and prevents the soil from subsiding around newly planted specimens. Then lightly rake again.

• Sprinkle over a general fertiliser like Growmore or pelleted chicken manure. Read the instructions and follow the application rate on the packet. Don't be tempted to add a little more – you'll do more harm than good. Then rake it in gently. Now you're ready for planting.

Aquilegia, Dicentra, candytuft, tulips & Ballota

LAYING OUT YOUR BORDERS

I always like to lay out my plants still in their pots before planting them. It allows me to check on what I've planned, and to ensure each plant has enough space. Remember to position them in threes, fives, sevens and nines. Even numbers are too linear and don't look natural. Odd numbers allow you to plant in different-sized 'triangles' and help break up straight lines; after all, your plants aren't soldiers on parade.

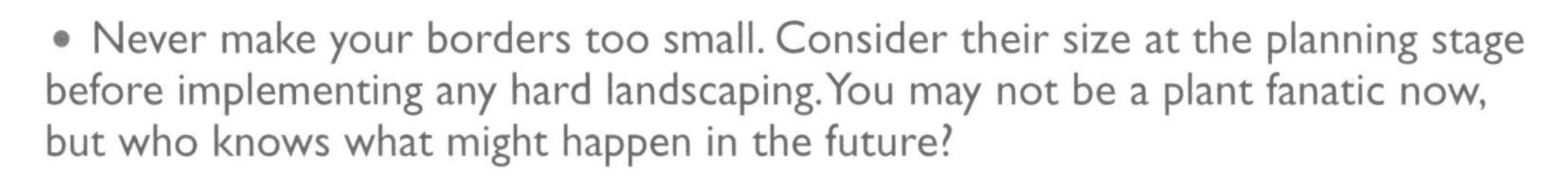

• Never make your borders too small. Consider their size at the planning stage before implementing any hard landscaping. You may not be a plant fanatic now, but who knows what might happen in the future?

• Small fiddly beds can be annoying, especially when lawns surround them – so many edges to trim. It's better to put in a few big ones, as long as they're in proportion with the garden. But don't make them so big that you can't easily access them for weeding and plant maintenance.

• Plan the size of the borders in sympathy with the other functions that the garden has to perform; you don't want the rotary dryer in the middle of your herbaceous border.

• Avoid narrow strips like the plague, especially if they're next to any boundaries. The bigger the border, the more plants you can play with. In some cases, you may want to rip the lawn up completely and devote the whole garden to wide borders that stretch across the plot – the essence of prairie planting.

HOW TO PLANT

• Dig a hole about twice the width of the rootball or the container that the plant has been growing in, and make it also about one-and-a-half times the depth. Fork over the bottom to loosen the soil.

• Sprinkle in a little fertiliser like bone meal or seaweed meal. These are high in phosphates to encourage root growth, and they also release their nutrients slowly to provide long-term nourishment to the roots. Slow-release fertilisers are often better than quick-release ones like dried blood, fishmeal, or hoof and horn, which can often lead to soft sappy growth.

• If your soil needs improving, mix it with peat-free multipurpose compost when back-filling the hole around the plant

• If the plant is bare-root, it will need staking. Drive the stake just off-centre so the roots can be fitted in around it. Don't ram a stake in after you've planted, or you'll go right through those precious roots! Stake on the windward side to reduce rubbing of the stem; use rubber ties to secure the stem.

• Ensure you put the plant in at the same depth as it was grown in the nursery. If it's too deep, the plant will suffocate; too shallow and the roots will dry out.

• Carefully fill the hole with soil, and firm it gently with your hands. If you are planting a large specimen in a big hole, then half-fill the hole and firm once, then continue filling and firm again. Mound up the soil around the plant to create a well, so that when you water, it doesn't all run away.

• Prune any dead or damaged wood back to just above a healthy bud and cut back by half any long straggly shoots.

• Water the plant thoroughly, then throw down a thick layer of mulch to reduce water evaporation, prevent weeds and to keep the soil warmer for longer.

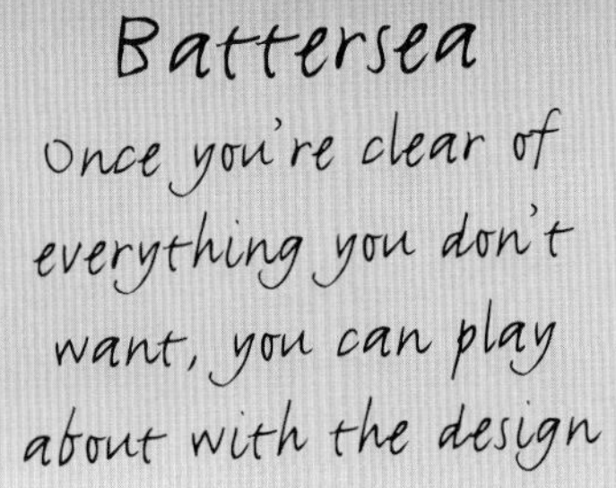

Battersea

Once you're clear of everything you don't want, you can play about with the design

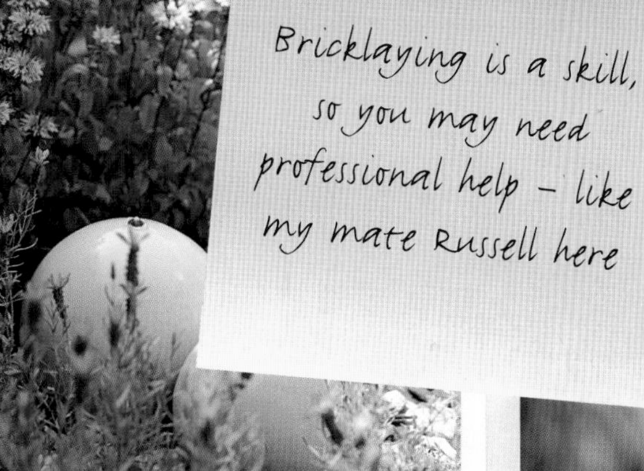
Bricklaying is a skill,
so you may need
professional help – like
my mate Russell here

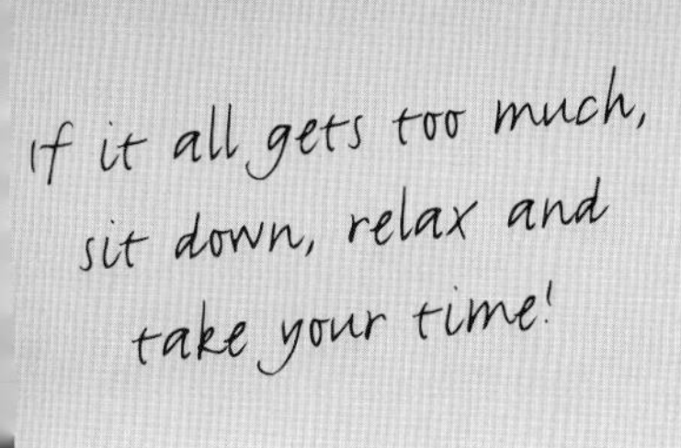
If it all gets too much,
sit down, relax and
take your time!

BATTERSEA

With its strong design features and a striking purple interior, Kath and Lee's house is a shrine to the '60s. As the couple are both out at work all day, they wanted a garden where they could chill out after work and at weekends – the focus was definitely on R&R, with plenty of sunbathing!

Although the space was fairly large for an urban garden, it was badly overlooked, so creating as much privacy as possible was my number one priority. To achieve this, I decided to sink the back lawn down into the garden, and surround it with tall grasses, perennials and a loquat (*Eriobotrya japonica*). This made the couple feel as if they were cocooned by the planting and hidden from prying eyes.

Lots of curves and strong lines are reflected throughout the design, with two teardrop-shaped lawns (very *Barbarella*, to complement the hanging cane chair!) edged in the same brick used to build the house. To continue the purple theme of the house interior, I introduced plants like Siberian iris, *Verbena bonariensis*, *Monarda* 'Beauty of Cobham' and *Cimicifuga simplex* Atropurpurea Group, to give lots of colour in spring and a real 'wow!' in the summer, when the garden was likely to be used the most.

The few evergreens dotted throughout the planting provide backbone to the overall scheme and interest in winter, as well as acting as a foil to seasonal planting.

WHAT GOES WHERE?

One of the most perplexing questions for any gardener is: 'Will this plant grow well here?' When you fancy sitting outside on a summer's evening after a day's work, which plants will soothe away your stress with their fabulous scent? What plants are suitable for groundcover? Or which climbers will do well on a shady north wall? Look no further! The following lists are designed to give you an idea of what will grow well in a particular environment in your garden. Remember, all plants will rocket away if they're in the right place.

TREES

Acacia dealbata

TREES TOLERANT OF HEAVY CLAY SOILS FOR SMALL GARDENS

• *Amelanchier lamarckii* (snowy mespilus) • *Corylus maxima* 'Purpurea' (purple filbert) • *Crataegus laevigata* 'Paul's Scarlet' (hawthorn) • *Crataegus oxycantha* 'Rosea Flore Pleno' (hawthorn) • *Laburnum* x *watereri* 'Vossii' • *Malus* 'Profusion' (crab apple) • *Malus* 'Red Jade' (crab apple) • *Pyrus salicifolia* 'Pendula' (silver pear) • *Prunus* 'Spire' (cherry) • *Salix babylonica* var. *pekinensis* 'Tortuosa' (corkscrew willow)

TREES FOR LIGHT, FREE-DRAINING SANDY SOILS FOR SMALL GARDENS

• *Acacia dealbata* (mimosa) • *Acer negundo* 'Variegatum' (box elder) • *Betula pendula* 'Purpurea' (purple silver birch) • *Cercidiphyllum japonicum* (candy floss tree) • *Cercis siliquastrum* (Judas tree) • *Gleditsia triacanthos* 'Ruby Lace' (honey locust) • *Laurus nobilis* (bay) • *Olea europaea* (olive) • *Robinia pseudoacacia* 'Tortuosa' • *Sophora japonica* (Japanese pagoda tree)

TREES TOLERANT OF VERY CHALKY SOILS

• *Acer negundo* 'Flamingo' (box elder) • *Albizia julibrissin* 'Rosea' (silk tree) • *Caragana arborescens* 'Pendula' (weeping pea tree) • *Crataegus laevigata* 'Paul's Scarlet' (hawthorn) • *Eucryphia* x *nymansensis* 'Nymansay' • *Euonymus europeaus* 'Red Cascade' (spindle tree) • *Hoheria* 'Glory of Amlwch' (lacebark) • *Malus* 'Evereste' (crab apple) • *Morus alba* 'Pendula' (weeping mulberry) • *Sorbus intermedia* (whitebeam)

TREES THAT PREFER ACID SOILS

• *Arbutus unedo* (strawberry tree) • *Cydonia oblonga* (quince) • *Embothrium coccineum* (Chilean fire bush) • *Halesia monticola* f. *vestita* (snowdrop tree) • *Hamamelis mollis* (Chinese witch hazel) • *Liquidambar orientalis* (sweet gum) • *Nyssa sinensis* (tupelo) • *Sorbus cashmiriana* (rowan) • *Stewartia sinensis* • *Styrax japonica* (Japanese snowball)

FRAGRANT TREES FOR SMALL GARDENS

• *Eucryphia* x *nymansensis* 'Nymansay' • *Hamamelis mollis* (Chinese witch hazel) • *Laburnum* x *watereri* 'Vossii' • *Luma apiculata* (myrtle) • *Magnolia* x *loebneri* 'Merrill' • *Malus* 'Golden Hornet' (crab apple) • *Malus* 'Profusion' (crab apple) • *Prunus* 'Amanogawa' (Japanese fastigiate cherry) • *Ptelea trifoliata* (hop tree) • *Styrax japonica* (Japanese snowball)

TREES WITH WINTER BARK FOR SMALL GARDENS

• *Acer davidii* 'Serpentine' (snake bark maple) • *Acer griseum* (paper bark maple) • *Acer pensylvanicum* 'Erythrocladum' (striped maple) • *Acer rufinerve* (snake bark maple) • *Betula albosinensis* var. *septentrionalis* (Chinese red birch) • *Betula pendula* 'Youngii' (Young's weeping birch) • *Prunus serrula* (Tibetan cherry)

TREES WITH STUNNING AUTUMN COLOUR FOR SMALL GARDENS

• *Acer capillipes* (snake bark maple) • *Acer japonicum* 'Vitifolium' (full moon maple) • *Amelanchier lamarckii* (snowy mespilus) • *Malus tschonoskii* (crab apple) • *Morus alba* 'Pendula' (weeping mulberry) • *Sorbus reducta* (rowan)

TREES FOR VERY SMALL GARDENS

• *Caragana arborescens* 'Pendula' (weeping pea tree) • *Mespilus germanica* 'Nottingham' (medlar) • *Morus alba* 'Pendula' (weeping mulberry) • *Prunus* 'Amanogawa' (fastigiate Japanese cherry) • *Prunus* 'Cheal's Weeping' (weeping Japanese cherry) • *Salix caprea* 'Pendula' (Kilmarnock willow)

ARCHITECTURAL SHRUBS FOR SUNNY SPOTS

• *Agave americana* 'Variegata' • *Cornus controversa* (wedding cake tree) • *Cupressus sempervirens* (Italian cypress) • *Euphorbia characias* subsp. *wulfenii* (spurge) • *Euphorbia mellifera* (honey spurge) • *Lupinus arboreus* (tree lupin) • *Phoenix canariensis* (Canary Island palm) • *Phormium tenax* (New Zealand flax) • *Sambucus racemosa* 'Sutherland Gold' (golden cut-leaved elderberry) • *Trachycarpus fortunei* (Chusan palm)

ARCHITECTURAL SHRUBS FOR SHADY SPOTS

• *Aucuba japonica* 'Rozannie' (Japanese laurel) • *Corylus avellana* 'Contorta' (corkscrew hazel) • *Fatsia japonica* 'Variegata' (Japanese aralia) • *Garrya elliptica* (silk tassel bush) • *Juniperus scopulorum* 'Skyrocket' (pencil juniper) • *Lonicera pileata* 'Maygrun' (shrubby honeysuckle) • *Pieris japonica* 'Forest Flame' • *Prunus laurocerasus* 'Otto Luyken' (cherry laurel) • *Skimmia japonica* 'Rubella' • *Viburnum davidii*

SHRUBS FOR GROUNDCOVER IN SUN

• *Artemisia* 'Powis Castle (wormwood) • *Ceanothus thyrsiflorus* var. *repens* (Californian lilac) • *Convolvulus cneorum* (shrubby bindweed) • *Daboecia cantabrica* (Irish heath) • *Daphne cneorum* (rose daphne) • *Erica carnea* (spring heath) • *Juniperus procumbens* 'Nana' (dwarf Japanese juniper) • *Rosa rugosa* var. *rosea* (pink hedgehog rose) • *Salvia officinalis* 'Purpurascens' (purple sage) • *Santolina chamaecyparissus* (cotton lavender)

SHRUBS TOLERANT OF DRY SHADE FOR GROUNDCOVER

• *Berberis wilsoniae* (barberry) • *Cornus canadensis* (creeping dogwood) • *Cotoneaster dammeri* 'Skogsholm' • *Euonymus fortunei* 'Emerald Gaiety' • *Hedera helix* 'Pittsburgh' (ivy) • *Hypericum calycinum* (rose of Sharon) • *Mahonia repens* • *Pachysandra terminalis* (Japanese spurge) • *Taxus baccata* 'Repandens' (spreading English yew) • *Vinca minor* (lesser periwinkle)

Convolvulus cneorum

SHRUBS

SHRUBS FOR LIGHT, FREE-DRAINING SANDY SOILS

• *Ceanothus thyrsiflorus* var. *repens* • *Cistus* x *corbariensis* (rock rose) • *Cytisus* 'Killiney Red' (broom) • *Genista lydia* (broom) • *Lavandula angustifolia* 'Hidcote' (lavender) • *Olearia* x *haastii* (daisy bush) • *Phlomis italica* • *Spartium junceum* (Spanish broom) • *Tamarix ramosissima* 'Pink Cascade' (tamarisk) • *Ulex europaeus* 'Flore Pleno' (gorse)

SHRUBS TOLERANT OF HEAVY CLAY SOILS

• *Aronia arbutifolia* (red chokeberry) • *Aucuba japonica* 'Rozannie' (spotted laurel) • *Berberis thunbergii* 'Aurea' (barberry) • *Chaenomeles* x *superba* 'Nicoline' (ornamental quince) • *Cornus alba* 'Sibirica' (dogwood) • *Cotoneaster* 'Coral Beauty' • *Forsythia suspensa* 'Nymans' • *Mahonia* x *media* 'Charity' • *Philadelphus* 'Avalanche' (mock orange) • *Viburnum opulus*

SHRUBS TOLERANT OF VERY CHALKY SOILS

• *Buddleia davidii* 'Nanaho Purple' (butterfly bush) • *Choisya ternata* 'Sundance' (Mexican orange blossom) • *Deutzia* x *rosea* • *Hypericum calycinum* (rose of Sharon) • *Philadelphus* 'Virginal' • *Phlomis fruticosa* (Jerusalem sage) • *Potentilla fruticosa* 'Daydawn' (cinquefoil) • *Rosa rugosa* 'Alba' (white hedgehog rose) • *Syringa meyeri* 'Palibin' (lilac) • *Viburnum tinus* 'Eve Price'

SHRUBS THAT PREFER ACID SOILS

• *Camellia* x *williamsii* 'Jury's Yellow' • *Cornus kousa* 'Chinensis ' (flowering dogwood) • *Corylopsis spicata* • *Enkianthus campanulatus* • *Hamamelis intermedia* 'Diane' (witch hazel) • *Kalmia latifolia* (calico bush) • *Leucothoe fontanesiana* 'Scarletta' • *Pieris japonica* 'White Cascade' • *Rhododendron* 'Dopey' • *Stachyurus praecox*

SCENTED SHRUBS FOR SHADY SPOTS

• *Abelia* x *grandiflora* • *Corylopsis spicata* • *Daphne odora* 'Aureomarginata' (winter *Daphne*) • *Lonicera* x *purpusii* 'Winter Beauty' (shrubby honeysuckle) • *Magnolia sieboldii* • *Mahonia aquifolium* (Oregon grape) • *Osmanthus* x *burkwoodii* • *Ribes odoratum* (buffalo currant) • *Sarcococca confusa* (Christmas box) • *Viburnum tinus* 'Eve Price'

SCENTED SHRUBS FOR SUNNY SPOTS

• *Buddleia alternifolia* (butterfly bush) • *Chimonanthus praecox* (wintersweet) • *Daphne* x *burkwoodii* • *Lavandula stoechas* (French lavender) • *Philadelphus* 'Belle Etoile' (mock orange) • *Pittosporum tobira* (Japanese mock orange) • *Poncirus trifoliata* (Japanese bitter orange) • *Rosmarinus officinalis* (common rosemary) • *Syringa microphylla* (dwarf lilac) • *Viburnum* x *juddii*

SHRUBS WITH STUNNING AUTUMN COLOUR

• *Acer palmatum* 'Dissectum' (cut-leaved Japanese maple) • *Acer palmatum* 'Osakazuki' (Japanese maple) • *Cornus mas* (Cornelian cherry) • *Cotinus coggygria* 'Flame' (smoke bush) • *Enkianthus campanulatus* • *Euonymus alatus* (winged spindle) • *Fothergilla monticola* • *Nandina domestica* 'Firepower' (heavenly bamboo) • *Ribes odoratum* (buffalo currant) • *Viburnum opulus* 'Roseum' (guelder rose)

SHRUBS · HEDGES

DECIDUOUS SHRUBS TOLERANT OF AIR POLLUTION

• *Buddleia davidii* 'Black Knight' (butterfly bush) • *Cornus stolonifera* 'Flaviramea' (dogwood) • *Philadelphus coronarius* 'Aureus' (mock orange) • *Physocarpus opulifolius* 'Diablo' (ninebark) • *Rosa rugosa* 'Sarah van Fleet' (pink hedgehog rose) • *Spiraea japonica* 'Goldflame' • *Syringa microphylla* (small-leaved lilac) • *Viburnum* x *carlesii* • *Viburnum opulus* (guelder rose) • *Weigela florida* 'Foliis Purpureis'

EVERGREEN SHRUBS TOLERANT OF AIR POLLUTION

• *Brachyglottis* 'Sunshine' • *Camellia japonica* 'Donation' • *Choisya ternata* 'Aztec Pearl' (Mexican orange blossom) • *Euonymus fortunei* 'Emerald 'n' Gold' • *Hypericum* 'Hidcote' (St John's wort) • *Lonicera pileata* 'Maygrun' (shrubby honeysuckle) • *Lavandula angustifolia* 'Hidcote Pink' (lavender) • *Mahonia aquifolium* 'Smaragd' (Oregon grape) • *Sarcococca hookeriana* 'Purple Stem' (Christmas box) • *Viburnum davidii*

PLANTS FOR FORMAL HEDGES

• *Carpinus betulus* (hornbeam) • *Chamaecyparis lawsoniana* (Lawson cypress) • *Crataegus monogyna* (hawthorn) • *Elaeagnus* x *ebbingei* • *Fagus sylvatica purpurea* (purple beech) • *Lonicera nitida* 'Baggesen's Gold' (shrubby honeysuckle) • *Prunus laurocerasus* (cherry laurel) • *Prunus lusitanica* (Portuguese laurel) • *Taxus baccata* (yew) • *Thuja plicata* (western red cedar)

SPIKY HEDGING PLANTS FOR SECURITY

• *Berberis darwinii* (barberry) • *Berberis thunbergii* 'Atropurpurea' (barberry) • *Crataegus monogyna* (hawthorn) • *Ilex aquifolium* 'Golden Milkboy' (holly) • *Ilex aquifolium* 'Handsworth New Silver' (holly) • *Mahonia* x *media* 'Charity' • *Osmanthus heterophyllus* (false holly) • *Prunus spinosa* (blackthorn) • *Pyracantha* 'Golden Charmer' (firethorn) • *Rosa eglanteria* (sweet briar)

FLOWERING SHRUBS FOR INFORMAL HEDGES

• *Deutzia* x *magnifica* • *Forsythia* x *intermedia* 'Lynwood' (golden bell) • *Fuchsia magellanica* 'Riccartonii' (hardy *Fuchsia*) • *Lonicera* x *purpusii* 'Winter Beauty' (winter honeysuckle) • *Rhododendron luteum* • *Ribes sanguineum* 'King Edward VII' (flowering currant) • *Rosa rugosa* 'Alba' (white hedgehog rose) • *Spiraea nipponica* 'Snowmound' • *Viburnum tinus* • *Weigela florida* 'Variegata'

SHRUBS FOR DWARF HEDGES

• *Berberis thunbergii* 'Atropurpurea Nana' (barberry) • *Buxus sempervirens* (box) • *Erica carnea* 'Springwood White' (heather) • *Hebe rakaiensis* (shrubby veronica) • *Ilex crenata* 'Convexa' (box-leaved holly) • *Lavandula angustifolia* 'Kew Red' (lavender) • *Pittosporum tenuifolium* 'Tom Thumb' • *Potentilla fruticosa* 'Royal Flush' (cinquefoil) • *Rosmarinus officinalis* 'Miss Jessopp's Upright' • *Santolina chamaecyparissus* (cotton lavender)

Santolina chamaecyparissus 'Lemon Queen'

CLIMBERS & WALL SHRUBS

SCENTED CLIMBERS & WALL SHRUBS FOR SUNNY WALLS & FENCES

• *Ceanothus* 'Puget's Blue' (Californian lilac) • *Clematis armandii* 'Snowdrift' (evergreen virgin's bower) • *Cytisus battandieri* (pineapple broom) • *Jasminum* x *stephanense* (jasmine) • *Lonicera periclymenum* 'Serotina' (honeysuckle) • *Passiflora caerulea* (passionflower) • *Rosa banksiae* 'Lutea' • *Trachelospermum jasminoides* (star jasmine) • *Vitax agnus-castus* (chaste tree) • *Wisteria floribunda* (Japanese wisteria)

SCENTED CLIMBERS & WALLS SHRUBS FOR SHADY WALLS & FENCES

• *Akebia quinata* (chocolate vine) • *Chaenomeles* 'Nivalis' (ornamental quince) • *Clematis montana* 'Pink Perfection' (virgin's bower) • *Clematis montana* var. *rubens* (virgin's bower) • *Clematis rehderiana* (virgin's bower) • *Lonicera japonica* 'Halliana' (Japanese honeysuckle)

FREE-CLIMBING PLANTS

• *Campsis radicans* (trumpet vine) • *Hedera canariensis* 'Gloire de Marengo' (Canary Island ivy) • *Hydrangea petiolaris* (climbing *Hydrangea*) • *Parthenocissus quinquefolia* (Virginia creeper) • *Parthenocissus tricuspidata* (Boston ivy) • *Schizophragma hydrangeoides* 'Roseum'

EVERGREEN CLIMBERS & WALL SHRUBS

• *Berberidopsis corallina* (coral plant) • *Clematis cirrhosa* var. *balearica* (evergreen virgin's bower) • *Garrya elliptica* 'James Roof' (silk tassel bush) • *Hedera helix* 'Hibernica' (ivy) • *Itea illicifolia* (sweetspire) • *Solanum jasminoides* 'Album' (potato vine) • *Trachelospermum jasminoides* (star jasmine)

CLIMBERS FOR TRAINING THROUGH EVERGREENS

• *Eccremocarpus scaber* (Chilean glory flower) • *Humulus lupulus* 'Aureus' (golden hop) • *Ipomoea lobata* (Spanish flag) • *Lathyrus latifolius* (everlasting sweet pea) • *Tropaeolum peregrinum* (canary creeper) • *Tropaeolum speciosum* (flame nasturtium)

OTHER CLIMBERS & WALL SHRUBS FOR SUNNY WALLS & FENCES

• *Abutilon megapotamicum* • *Actinidia kolomikta* (kiwi) • *Aristolochia macrophylla* (Dutchman's pipe) • *Campsis* x *tagliabuana* (trumpet vine) • *Clematis* 'Beauty of Worcester' (virgin's bower) • *Clematis* 'Etoile Violette' (virgin's bower) • *Lonicera periclymenum* 'Belgica' (Dutch honeysuckle) • *Solanum crispum* 'Glasnevin' (potato vine) • *Vitis vinifera* 'Brant' (grape vine) • *Wisteria floribunda* 'Rosea' (Japanese *Wisteria*)

OTHER CLIMBERS & WALL SHRUBS FOR SHADY WALLS & FENCES

• *Berberidopsis corallina* (coral plant) • *Clematis* 'Nelly Moser' (virgin's bower) • *Clematis macropetala* 'Markham's' Pink' (virgin's bower) • *Cotoneaster horizontalis* (fishbone *Cotoneaster*) • *Hedera helix* 'Sagittifolia' (ivy) • *Humulus lupulus* 'Aureus' (golden hop) • *Jasminum nudiflorum* (winter jasmine) • *Lonicera* x *tellmanniana* (honeysuckle) • *Rosa* 'Climbing Iceberg' • *Rosa* 'Zéphirine Drouhine'

Wisteria floribunda

PERENNIALS

ARCHITECTURAL PERENNIALS FOR SUNNY SPOTS

• *Allium giganteum* (ornamental onion) • *Crocosmia* 'Lucifer' (montbretia) • *Cimicifuga simplex* Atropurpurea Group • *Cynara cardunculus* (globe artichoke) • *Echinops ritro* (globe thistle) • *Eryngium giganteum* (Miss Willmott's ghost) • *Iris pallida* 'Variegata' • *Lilium candidum* (Madonna lily) • *Macleaya cordata* (plume poppy) • *Verbascum olympicum* (mullein)

ARCHITECTURAL PERENNIALS FOR SHADY SPOTS

• *Acanthus mollis* (bear's breeches) • *Angelica atropurpurea* • *Astilboides tabularis* • *Digitalis purpurea* f. *albiflora* (white foxglove) • *Gunnera manicata* (giant rhubarb) • *Helleborus argutifolius* (Christmas rose) • *Hosta sieboldiana* var. *elegans* (plantain lily) • *Ligularia stenocephala* 'The Rocket' • *Rheum palmatum* 'Atrosanguineum' (ornamental rhubarb) • *Rodgersia aesculifolia*

PERENNIALS FOR GROUNDCOVER IN DAMP SHADE

• *Alchemilla mollis* (lady's mantle) • *Asarum europaeum* (European wild ginger) • *Blechnum spicant* (hard fern) • *Brunnera macrophylla* (Siberian bugloss) • *Hosta* 'Sum and Substance' (plantain lily) • *Primula florindae* (giant cowslip) • *Houttuynia cordata* 'Chameleon' • *Lamium maculatum* 'White Nancy' (spotted dead nettle) • *Omphalodes verna* (blue-eyed Mary) • *Tellima grandiflora* 'Purpurea' (fringe cups)

PERENNIALS FOR GROUNDCOVER TOLERANT OF DRY SHADE

• *Ajuga reptans* 'Burgundy Glow' (bugle) • *Bergenia cordifolia* 'Purpurea' (elephant's ears) • *Convallaria majalis* (lily of the valley) • *Epimedium* x *rubrum* • *Geranium macrorrhizum* (cranesbill) • *Geum* 'Mrs Bradshaw' (avens) • *Lysimachia nummularia* 'Aurea' (creeping Jenny) • *Prunella vulgaris* 'Pagoda' (self-heal) • *Tiarella cordifolia* (foam flower) • *Waldsteinia ternata* (barren strawberry)

PERENNIALS FOR GROUNDCOVER IN FULL SUN

• *Aubrieta* 'Carnival' (aubrieta) • *Cerastium tomentosum* (snow-in-summer) • *Diascia* 'Salmon Supreme' • *Helianthemum* 'Wisley Primrose' (rock rose) • *Lamium maculatum* 'Beacon Silver' (dead nettle) • *Papaver orientale* 'Perry's White' (poppy) • *Santolina pinnata* subsp. *neapolitana* • *Sedum telephium* 'Matrona' (ice plant) • *Silene hookeri* (campion) • *Stachys byzantina* 'Silver Carpet' (lamb's ears)

MIDDLE TO BACK OF BORDER PERENNIALS FOR SUN (OVER 1M/3FT TALL)

• *Agapanthus* 'Blue Giant' (African blue lily) • *Asphodeline lutea* (king's spear) • *Crambe cordifolia* • *Delphinium elatum* 'Bruce' • *Eremurus robustus* (foxtail lily) • *Helianthus* x *multiflorus* (perennial sunflower) • *Kniphofia* 'Fiery Fred' (red hot poker) • *Sidalcea* 'Croftway Red' (prairie mallow) • *Solidago* 'Golden Wings' (golden rod) • *Verbascum olympicum* (mullein)

PERENNIALS

MIDDLE TO BACK OF BORDER PERENNIALS FOR SHADE (OVER1M/3FT TALL)

• *Acanthus mollis* (bear's breeches) • *Aconitum napellus* (monkshood) • *Angelica archangelica* • *Aruncus dioicus* 'Kneiffii' • *Campanula lactiflora* 'Loddon Anna' • *Filipendula rubra* (meadow sweet) • *Macleaya microcarpa* 'Coral Plume' (plume poppy) • *Rheum palmatum* 'Bowles' Crimson' (ornamental rhubarb) • *Rodgersia aesculifolia* • *Smilacina racemosa* (false spikenard)

PERENNIALS TOLERANT OF HEAVY CLAY SOILS

• *Anemone hupehensis* var. *japonica* (Japanese anemone) • *Aster novi-belgii* 'Kristina' (michaelmas daisy) • *Astrantia major* 'Hadspen Blood' (masterwort) • *Cimicifuga simplex* Atropurpurea Group • *Eupatorium purpureum* 'Atropurpureum' • *Inula hookeri* • *Lysimachia ciliata* 'Firecracker' (loosestrife) • *Persicaria bistorta* 'Superba' • *Prunella vulgaris* 'Pagoda' (self-heal) • *Pulmonaria saccharata* (lungwort)

PERENNIALS FOR LIGHT, FREE-DRAINING SANDY SOILS

• *Asphodeline lutea* (king's spear) • *Chrysanthemum maximum* • *Dictamnus albus* var. *purpureus* • *Geum* 'Lady Stratheden' (avens) • *Euphorbia amygdaloides* 'Purpurea' (wood spurge) • *Lupinus* 'Chandelier' (lupin) • *Lysimachia ciliata* 'Firecracker' • *Symphytum grandiflorum* (comfrey) • *Pulsatilla vulgaris* • *Artemisia ludoviciana* (white sage)

SCENTED PERENNIALS FOR SUNNY SPOTS

• *Agastache foeniculum* (anise hyssop) • *Artemisia* 'Powis Castle' • *Cosmos atrosanguineus* (chocolate cosmos) • *Crambe cordifolia* • *Dianthus* 'Lavender Clove' (pink) • *Erysimum cheiri* (perennial wallflower) • *Hemerocallis citrina* (day lily) • *Paeonia lactiflora* (peony) • *Phlox maculata* (meadow phlox) • *Salvia glutinosa* (Jupiter's distaff)

Echinops ritro

SCENTED PERENNIALS FOR SHADY SPOTS

• *Convallaria majalis* (lily of the valley) • *Geranium endressii* (cranesbill) • *Geranium macrorrhizum* (cranesbill) • *Helleborus foetidus* (Christmas rose) • *Hosta* 'Honeybells' (plantain lily) • *Iris foetidissima* var. *citrina* (roast beef iris) • *Iris unguicularis* (Algerian iris) • *Lunaria rediviva* (perennial honesty) • *Nepeta* x *faassenii* 'Six Hills Giant' (catmint) • *Primula veris* (primrose)

PERENNIALS WITH DECORATIVE SEED HEADS IN WINTER

• *Achillea filipendulina* (ornamental yarrow) • *Agapanthus* Headbourne hybrids • *Cynara cardunculus* (globe artichoke) • *Echinops ritro* (globe thistle) • *Eupatorium purpureum* 'Atropurpureum' • *Monarda* 'Beauty of Cobham' (bergamot) • *Phlomis tuberosa* • *Rudbeckia fulgida* var. *sullivantii* 'Goldstrum' (coneflower) • *Sedum spectabile* 'Autumn Joy' (ice plant) • *Verbena bonariensis*

PERENNIALS · GRASSES

Liatris spicata

PERENNIALS THAT READILY SELF-SEED

• *Alchemilla mollis* (lady's mantle) • *Anthriscus sylvestris* (cow parsley) • *Eryngium planum* (sea holly) • *Geranium phaeum* (cranesbill) • *Lychnis chalcedonica* (Jerusalem cross) • *Lythrum virgatum* 'The Rocket' (loosestrife) • *Pimpinella major* 'Rosea' • *Polemonium caeruleum* (Jacob's ladder) • *Pulmonaria officinalis* (lungwort) • *Thalictrum delavayi* (meadow rue)

PERENNIALS TOLERANT OF AIR POLLUTION

• *Achillea* 'Summer Wine' (ornamental yarrow) • *Anemone* x *hybrida* 'Honorine Jobert' (Japanese *Anemone*) • *Artemisia ludoviciana* (white sage) • *Crocosmia* 'Lucifer' (montbretia) • *Hemerocallis* 'Atun' (day lily) • *Heuchera* 'Chocolate Ruffles' • *Liatris spicata* (gay feather) • *Lupinus* 'Chandelier' (lupin) • *Veronicastrum virginicum* f. *album* (culvers root) • *Veronica spicata* 'Sightseeing' (ironweed)

PERENNIALS FOR PLANTING IN LARGE DRIFTS

• *Achillea* 'Gold Plate' (ornamental yarrow) • *Aster novi-belgii* 'Royal Ruby' (michaelmas daisy) • *Cirsium rivulare* 'Atropurpureum' (plumed thistle) • *Echinacea* 'White Swan' (coneflower) • *Eryngium* x *oliverianum* (sea holly) • *Gaura* 'Siskiyou Pink' • *Helenium* 'Moorheim Beauty' (Helen's flower) • *Lilium henryi* (lily) • *Lysimachia ciliata* 'Firecracker' (loosestrife) • *Verbena hastata* 'Rosea'

VERY QUICK GROWING, VIGOROUS PERENNIALS

• *Epilobium angustifolium* f. *album* (willow herb) • *Euphorbia amygdaloides* var. *robbiae* (wood spurge) • *Euphorbia griffithii* 'Fireglow' (spurge) • *Geranium nodosum* (cranesbill) • *Lysimachia clethroides* (loosestrife) • *Lysimachia punctata* (dotted loosestrife) • *Persicaria bistorta* (knotweed) • *Physalis alkekengi* var. *franchetii* (Chinese lantern) • *Physostegia virginiana* 'Summer Snow' (obedient plant) • *Trachystemon orientalis*

GRASSES FOR DAMP/MOIST SITES

• *Acorus calamus* (sweet flag) • *Carex elata* 'Aurea' (Bowles' golden sedge) • *Carex grayi* (Gray's sedge) • *Carex pendula* (weeping sedge) • *Luzula nivea* (snowy woodrush) • *Luzula sylvatica* (greater woodrush) • *Panicum virgatum* (switch grass) • *Poa chaixii* (broad-leaved meadow grass) • *Spartina pectinata* 'Aureomarginata' (prairie cord grass) • *Uncinia rubra* (hook sedge)

GRASSES TOLERANT OF HOT/DRY SITES

• *Bouteloua gracilis* (mosquito grass) • *Briza media* (perennial quaking grass) • *Carex buchananii* (red fox sedge) • *Cortaderia selloana* 'Pumila' (dwarf pampas grass) • *Festuca glauca* 'Elijah Blue' (blue fescue) • *Helictotrichon sempervirens* (blue oat grass) • *Koeleria glauca* (blue hairgrass) • *Melica ciliata* • *Stipa gigantea* (giant feather grass) • *Stipa tenuissima* (feather grass)

GRASSES·ANNUALS & BIENNIALS

Arundo donax

SHADE-TOLERANT GRASSES

• *Carex* 'Evergold' (variegated golden sedge) • *Carex muskingumensis* (palm leaf sedge) • *Carex pendula* (weeping sedge) • *Deschampsia flexuosa* (crinkled hairgrass) • *Hystrix patula* (bottlebrush grass) • *Luzula nivea* (snowy woodrush) • *Melica altissima* 'Atropurpurea' (Siberian melic) • *Phalaris arundinacea* 'Picta' (gardener's garters) • *Sorghastrum nutans* (Indian grass) • *Uniola latifolia* (wild oats)

TALL GRASSES FOR SUN/LIGHT SHADE

• *Arundo donax* (giant reed) • *Calamagrostis* x *acutiflora* 'Karl Foerster' (reed grass) • *Miscanthus sacchariflorus* (silver banner grass) • *Miscanthus sinensis* (Chinese silver grass) • *Miscanthus sinensis* 'Flamingo' (Chinese silver grass) • *Miscanthus sinensis* 'Gracillimus' (Chinese silver grass) • *Miscanthus sinensis* 'Silberfeder' (Chinese silver grass) • *Miscanthus sinensis* 'Strictus' (tiger grass) • *Panicum virgatum* 'Heavy Metal' (switch grass) • *Stipa gigantea* (giant feather grass)

GROUNDCOVER GRASSES

• *Carex buchananii* (red fox sedge) • *Deschampsia cespitosa* (tufted hair grass) • *Festuca glauca* 'Blaufuchs' (blue fescue) • *Hakonechloa macra* 'Aureola' • *Imperata cylindrica* 'Rubra' (Japanese blood grass) • *Luzula nivea* (snowy woodrush) • *Molinia caerulea* subsp. *arundinacea* (purple moor grass) • *Pennisetum orientale* (fountain grass) • *Pennisetum setaceum* 'Rubrum' (purple fountain grass) • *Saccharum ravennae* (Ravenna grass)

GRASSES FOR PLANTING IN LARGE DRIFTS

• *Deschampsia cespitosa* 'Goldtau' (hair grass) • *Deschampsia flexuosa* 'Tatra Gold' (wavy hair grass) • *Hordeum jubatum* (squirrel tail grass) • *Imperata cylindrica* 'Rubra' (Japanese blood grass) • *Miscanthus sinensis* 'Flamingo' (Chinese silver grass) • *Panicum virgatum* 'Rehbrawn' (switch grass) • *Pennisetum alopecuroides* 'Little Bunny' (fountain grass) • *Poa chaixii* (broad-leaved meadow grass) • *Stipa calamagrostis* (feather grass) • *Stipa tenuisssima* (feather grass)

TALL ARCHITECTURAL ANNUALS & BIENNIALS

• *Alcea rosea* (hollyhock) • *Amaranthus* var. *viridis* 'Green Tails' (love-lies-bleeding) • *Centaurea cyanus* (cornflower) • *Cleome hassleriana* • *Digitalis purpurea* f. *albiflora* (white foxglove) • *Helianthus annuus* (sun flower) • *Kochia scoparia* • *Nigella damascena* (love-in-a-mist) • *Ricinus communis* (castor oil plant) • *Verbascum bombyciferum* (mullein)

CLIMBING ANNUALS

• *Cobaea scandens* f. *alba* (cathedral cup) • *Ipomoea tricolor* 'Heavenly Blue' (morning glory) • *Lathyrus odoratus* (sweet pea) • *Thunbergia alata* (black-eyed Susan) • *Tropaeolum majus* Whirlybird Series (nasturtium) • *Tropaeolum peregrinum* (nasturtium)

WATER PLANTS·HERBS

POND PLANTS – SHALLOW MARGINALS (15CM/6IN WATER)

• *Acorus gramineus* 'Ogon' • *Calla palustris* (bog arum) • *Caltha palustris* 'Flore Pleno' • *Houttuynia cordata* 'Chameleon' (marsh marigold) • *Juncus effusus* f. *spiralis* (corkscrew rush) • *Lysichiton americanus* (skunk cabbage) • *Mentha aquatica* (watermint) • *Mimulus cardinalis* (scarlet monkey flower) • *Sparganium natans* (burr reed) • *Typha minima* (bulrush)

POND PLANTS – DEEP MARGINALS (30CM/12IN WATER)

• *Alisma plantago-aquatica* (water plantain) • *Cyperus papyrus* (Egyptian paper rush) • *Glyceria maxima* 'Variegata' • *Hottonia palustris* (water violet) • *Iris pseudacorus* 'Golden Fleece' (yellow flag *Iris*) • *Nelumbo nucifera* 'Alba Stricta' (lotus) • *Ranunculus lingua* 'Grandiflora' (greater spearwort) • *Typha angustifolia* (lesser bulrush) • *Typha latifolia* 'Variegata' (bulrush) • *Zantedeschia aethiopica* 'Green Goddess' (arum lily)

DEEP WATER PLANTS (30–100CM/1–3FT WATER)

• *Aponogeton distachyos* (water hawthorn) • *Nuphar lutea* (yellow pond lily) • *Nymphaea* 'Virginalis' (water lily) • *Nymphaea* 'Sunrise' (water lily) • *Nymphoides indica* (water snowflake) • *Orontium aquaticum* (golden club)

BOG PLANTS (HERBACEOUS PERENNIALS TOLERANT OF VERY WET SOIL)

• *Astilbe chinensis* var. *davidii* • *Lobelia cardinalis* 'Queen Victoria' • *Hosta* 'Blue Angel' (plantain lily) • *Iris laevigata* 'Rosea' • *Iris siberica* f. *alba* • *Leucojum aestivum* (summer snowflake) • *Ligularia przewalskii* • *Lythrum salicaria* 'Firecandle' (purple loosestrife) • *Primula denticulata* (drumstick primrose) • *Trollius europaeus* 'Canarybird' (common European globeflower)

PERENNIAL HERBS FOR DRY SUN

• *Artemisia dracunculus* (French tarragon) • *Helichrysum italicum* (curry plant) • *Laurus nobilis* (bay) • *Rosmarinus officinalis* (rosemary) • *Salvia officinalis* (sage) • *Thymus vulgaris* (thyme)

PERENNIAL HERBS FOR MOIST SHADE

• *Allium schoenoprasum* (chives) • *Melissa officinalis* (lemon balm) • *Levisticum officinale* (lovage) • *Mentha* (mint) • *Monarda didyma* (bergamot) • *Myrrhis odorata* (sweet cicely)

ANNUAL/BIENNIAL HERBS FOR SUN

• *Anethum graveolens* (dill) • *Anthriscus cerefolium* (chervil) • *Carum carvi* (caraway) • *Coriandrum sativum* (coriander) • *Ocimum basilicum* (sweet basil) • *Petroselinum crispum* (parsley)

Laurus nobilis

ODDS & SODS

PLANTS FOR EVENING SCENT

• *Daphne odora* 'Aureomarginata' (winter *Daphne*) • *Datura arborea* (angel's trumpet) • *Ipomoea alba* (moonflower) • *Jasminum officinale* (common jasmine) • *Lilium candidum* (Madonna lily) • *Lilium regale* (regal lily) • *Lilium* 'Pink Perfection' (lily) • *Matthiola bicornis* (night-scented stock) • *Oenothera biennis* (evening primrose) • *Zaluzianskya capensis*

TOUGH, FRAGRANT ROSES

• *Rosa* 'Charles de Mills' (crimson pink Gallica rose) • *Rosa* 'Comte de Chambord' (bright pink Portland rose) • *Rosa* 'Comtesse du Caÿla' (salmon China rose) • *Rosa* 'Cuisse de Nymphe' (pink Alba rose) • *Rosa gallica* 'Versicolor' (crimson with white streaks) • *Rosa* 'Ispahan' (pink Damask rose) • *Rosa* 'Little White Pet' (white Polyantha rose) • *Rosa* 'Reine des Violettes' (purple Hybrid perpetual) • *Rosa rugosa* 'Alba' (white hedgehog rose) • *Rosa rugosa* 'Roseraie de l'Haÿ' (crimson-purple hedgehog rose)

LARGE FERNS FOR DAMP SHADE

• *Dicksonia antarctica* (tree fern) • *Dryopteris affinis* 'Cristata' (golden male fern) • *Matteuccia struthiopteris* (shuttlecock fern) • *Osmunda regalis* (royal fern) • *Polystichum munitum* (sword fern) • *Polystichum setiferum* 'Plumosomultilobum' (soft shield fern)

Rosa rugosa

SMALL FERNS FOR DAMP SHADE

• *Adiantum pedatum* (maidenhair fern) • *Asplenium scolopendrium* (hart's tongue fern) • *Athyrium filix-femina* (female fern) • *Athyrium nipponicum* var. *pictum* (Japanese painted fern) • *Blechnum spicant* (hard fern) • *Polypodium vulgare* (common polypody)

WELL-BEHAVED BAMBOOS FOR THE SMALL GARDEN

• *Chusquea coronalis* • *Fargesia nitida* (fountain bamboo) • *Fargesia murielae* (umbrella bamboo) • *Phyllostachys nigra* f. *henonis* (black bamboo) • *Pleioblastus pygmaeus* (pygmy bamboo) • *Fargesia nitida* 'Nymphenburg'

LARGE SPREADING BAMBOOS FOR SCREENING/HEDGES

• *Arundinaria anceps* • *Arundo donax* (giant reed) • *Phyllostachys bissetii* • *Phyllostachys nigra* (black bamboo) • *Phyllostachys viridiglaucescens* • *Pseudosasa japonica*

ODDS & SODS

Sorbus cashmiriana

FRAGRANT BULBS

• *Amaryllis belladonna* (belladonna lily) • *Cardiocrinum giganteum* (Himalayan lily) • *Crocus* 'E. A. Bowles' • *Galanthus nivalis* (snowdrop) • *Galtonia candicans* (Cape hyacinth) • *Hyacinthoides non-scripta* (bluebell) • *Iris reticulata* • *Narcissus jonquilla* (jonquil) • *Narcissus poeticus* 'Plenus' (poet's *Narcissus*) • *Tulipa sylvestris* (dwarf tulip)

BULBS FOR CONTAINERS

• *Colchicum autumnale* 'Roseum Plenum' (autumn crocus) • *Crocus* 'Joan of Arc' • *Fritillaria imperialis* 'Maxima Lutea' (crown imperial) • *Hyacinthus* 'Delft Blue' (Dutch hyacinth) • *Lilium longiflorum* (Easter lily) • *Muscari botryoides* 'Album' (grape hyacinth) • *Narcissus* 'Golden Harvest' (large-flowered daffodil) • *Narcissus* 'Ice King' (double-flowered daffodil) • *Nectaroscordum siculum* • *Tulipa* 'Dr Plesman' (tulip)

TREES & SHRUBS WITH BERRIES TO ATTRACT BIRDS

• *Cotoneaster frigidus* • *Crataegus laevigata* 'Paul's Scarlet' (hawthorn) • *Daphne mezereum* • *Ilex aquifolium* 'J. C. van Tol' (holly) • *Leycesteria formosa* (Himalayan honeysuckle) • *Mahonia aquifolium* (Oregon grape) • *Malus* 'John Downie' (crab apple) • *Sorbus cashmiriana* (Kashmir rowan) • *Sorbus reducta* (rowan) • *Viburnum opulus* 'Roseum' (guelder rose)

PLANTS TO ATTRACT BUTTERFLIES

• *Allium* 'Globemaster' (ornamental onion) • *Buddleia davidii* 'Royal Red' (butterfly bush) • *Escallonia* 'Apple Blossom' • *Inula hookeri* • *Lavandula stoechas* (French lavender) • *Monarda* 'Beauty of Cobham' (bergamot) • *Rubus cockburnianus* • *Salvia nemorosa* 'East Friesland' (sage) • *Syringa microphylla* (lilac) • *Thymus vulgaris* (thyme)

DECORATIVE & EDIBLE VEGETABLES

Beetroot: 'Bull's Blood' • Chicory: 'Red Verona', 'Vesuvio' • Curly kale: 'Redbor' • Endive (curled-leaf lettuce variety) • Fennel (bulb variety) • French bean (dwarf): 'Royalty' • Lettuce: 'Lollo Rosso', 'Catalogna', 'Little Gem' • Mibuna (Japanese greens) • Mizuna (Japanese greens) • Pak choi: 'Tah Tsai' • Pea: 'Purple Podded' • Pumpkin: 'Turk's Turban' • Rocket • Runner bean (climbing): 'Scarlet Emperor', 'Painted Lady', 'Sunset' • Runner bean (dwarf): 'Hestia' • Swiss chard: 'Charlotte' • Tomato: 'Tumbler' (for hanging baskets and window boxes), 'Gardener's Delight' (cherry tomato) • Winter purslane • Winter squash: 'Jack be Little'

Glasgow
Arghhhhh! What a mess – but loads of mature plants worth keeping

Anything can be used as a focal point. This interesting tree stump cost only £8!

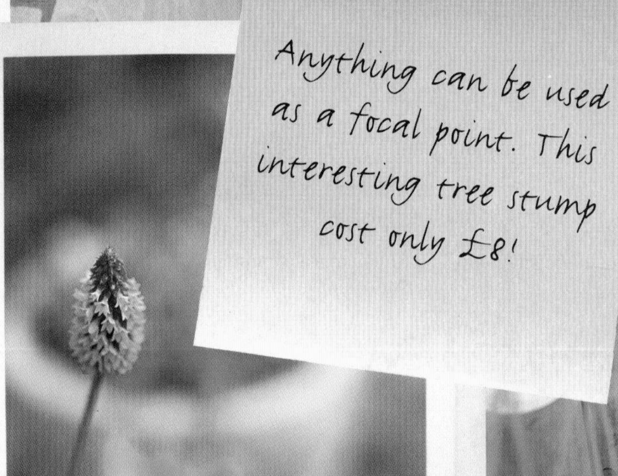

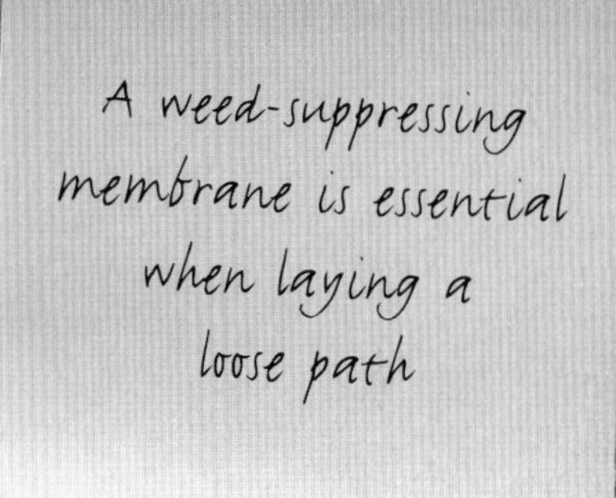

A weed-suppressing membrane is essential when laying a loose path

GLASGOW

Sharon and Gordon needed a child-friendly garden for their two kids, Jack and Connie. They wanted a lawn but didn't want the garden to look like a football pitch. As Sharon was at home part of the day, she wanted a space that held year-round interest. The garden itself sloped from left to right, and faced east, so it did get some sun but not much.

To deal with the difficult slope (and avoid expensive retaining walls), I created a tumbling hillock that sloped down to a level sandstone patio in one corner, and edged it with timber of different heights to retain the soil where needed. Lomond boulders and cobbles add texture and interest around the edges of a pebble path. In the opposite corner I made a small sunken seating area under the shadow of a red-berried rowan. Over the entrances to the sunken hideaway, the metal arches add an all-important vertical element and, when covered in ivy planted at the base, will make the corner even more intimate. Among the key evergreens, like *Skimmia japonica* 'Rubella', *Prunus laurocerasus* 'Otto Luyken', *Lonicera pileata* 'Maygrun' and *Nandina domestica*, there is a mixture of classic 'woodland' plants like *Hosta*, ferns, *Primula*, *Pulmonaria*, *Anemone* and *Helleborus foetidus*, all of which are ideal for Sharon as she wanted a 'woodland fairy feel'. The overall effect is naturally subtle, and will become more so when the timber starts to mellow with age.

INDEX

ACKNOWLEDGEMENTS

Special thanks to Helen and Alison for their tireless enthusiasm and hard work. My publishers HarperCollins, especially those with their hands in the mixer this time: Angela, Luke, Alastair and Lisa. Also Sharon and Hilary. Nikki for great photographs. TwoFour and *The City Gardener* team who worked so incredibly hard on the series. Russ and Tommy B for the laughs and advice. Jo and Ben at Channel 4. Ali, Julian and Jo at Curtis Brown. NESCOT, especially my friends in the Horticulture Department. Mrs F. Celia, Diana *et al* at Flittons Nursery. Tendercare, especially Richard and Craig. Matt at Outer Eden. All at Privett Garden Products. Tom, Dad, Lina, and the rest of my family. My buddies. Rachel King and Kevin for their relentless support and hard graft. And Ellie – thanks for helping me breathe occasionally.

The publishers would like to thank:

Nikki English
Everybody at TwoFour Productions
Kath Ludlow and Lee Murphy
Donald and Ann Jameson

Julia Ryan, Capel Manor, Bullsmoor Lane, Enfield, Middlesex EN1 4RQ

Andrew Hawksworth, Tendercare Nurseries, Southlands Road, Denham, Uxbridge, Middlesex UB9 4HD

Simon Haynes, Clifton Nurseries, 5a Clifton Villas, Little Venice, London W9 2PH

David Richardson
CP Ceramics, 150 Columbia Road, London E2 7RG

Fulham Palace Garden Centre, Bishops Avenue, London SW6. All profits from the garden centre go to the charity Fairbridge, which supports inner city youth.

PICTURE CREDITS

All photographs taken by Nikki English, except for the following:

Garden Picture Library
p45, p118T, p145M (David Cavagnaro), p163B (Juliette Wade)

John Glover
p37, p43, p107B, p120T, p133T, p138B, p141B

Matt James
p106M, p109T, p112M, p113M, p118M, p120M, p125M, p125T, p127M, p132M, p133B, p139M, p139B, p140 (all), p141M, p147B, p150T, p151B, p153M, p159M, p186, p188 (all), p194, p196

Photos Horticultural
p39, p40 (all), p42, p44, p47, p52, p55, p63 (PH/Stonemarket/Stuart Jones Copper Work), p67 (PH/Brinsbury Coll), p72 (PH/Shaw Trust/Designer: Caroline Simpson), p80, p89 (PH/Station Hse Cambridge), p108T, p109M, p112T, p114T, p119M, p120B, p121M, p124B, p125B, p126T, p126M, p127T, p132T, p132B, p133M, p135T, p138T, p144T, p145B, p146T, p147M, p152T, p153T, p157T, p162M, p165M, p172 (PH/Anglesey Abbey NT), p176, p179, p180 (Laurent-Perrier Harpers & Queen Garden designed by Tom Stuart-Smith at Chelsea FS 2001 – Gold Medal), p187

Tim Sandall
p46, p90, 106T, p106B, p107T, p107M, p108M, p108B, p109B, p112B, p114B, p115M, p115B, p117, p118B, p119T, p121T, p121B, p124T, p135M, p138M, p139T, p141T, p143, p144M, p144B, p145T, p146M, p146B, p147T, p150M, p150B, p151T, p151M, p152M, p152B, p153B, p156T, p156M, p156B, p157M, p157B, p158T, p158M, p158B, p159T, p159B, p162T, p162B, p163T, p163M, p164 (all), p165T, p165B, p181, p183L&R, p189, p204, p205, p207, p208, p209, p210, p211, p212, p214, p215

Chris Shaw
p113T, p114M, p115T, p124M, p127B

TwoFour Productions
p166TL, p166TR, p167TL